W9-CYH-216

Vigilante Woman

VIGILANTE WOMAN

by

Virginia Rowe Towle

South Brunswick

New York: A.S. Barnes and Co., Inc.

London: Thomas Yoseloff Ltd

© 1966 by A.S. Barnes and Co., Inc.
Library of Congress Catalogue Card Number: 66-21603

A.S. Barnes and Co., Inc.
South Brunswick, New Jersey

Thomas Yoseloff Ltd
18 Charing Cross Road
London W.C. 2, England

6247
Printed in the United States of America

FOR
Ted, Dorothy, and Frank, who urged me to
"Go Western"

Author's Note and Acknowledgments

It's almost impossible to give recognition to and express appreciation for all source material in *Vigilante Woman* because my research covered a span of more than seventeen years!

This adventure in researching started at the New York Public Library when Mr. Sylvester L. Vigilante (how prophetic his name was for me) suggested that I do a book on Libby Smith Collins, "The Cattle Queen of Montana." Immediately he guided me to the Library's Rare Book Section where he chained a copy of Mrs. Collins' book *The Cattle Queen of Montana or The Cowboys' Mother* to a desk. That book in turn chained me to the desk for some weeks of studying and research.

As Mr. Vigilante and I talked, Mrs. Collins' book became a mere prelude to our decision that I should do a book on several plucky pioneer women who were in Bannack or Virginia City, Montana, during the Montana Vigilante reign of 1863-1864.

Soon after the discovery of this rare old volume, I and my late husband, Courtenay Terrett, New York newspaper reporter and editor, Hollywood playwright, foreign correspondent, and author (*Only Saps Work,* Vanguard Press;

The White Cheyenne, Dodd-Mead), left New York City. Mr. Terrett was bound for Montana to do research on two books, a play, and several magazine pieces. I helped him with his research, often taking time out to jot down a few notes on the Vigilante Woman, who was always with me.

For some years after Mr. Terrett's death, I was absorbed in earning my living by newspaper, publicity, and advertising work in California, Alaska, New York, Nevada, Montana, and Washington. I never, however, entirely forgot the Vigilante Woman. In each city, I spent my leisure hours at the Public Library, reading background material, searching out information on my ever-present, courageous companions, these frontier women.

Finally, six years ago it was Montana re-visited. I once again made the Vigilante Woman, her modes and mores, her gallant days and ways, my primary theme.

During those years that I worked in faraway places, from Alaska to California to New York, I had scribbled down a sentence here, found a morsel there, for my book. Referring to these notes when I began actual work on the book, I found them on yellowed paper; many of them did not have the sources marked, but each one fitted into my story.

One revelation that grew out of my many years' research is very precious to me: the realization that librarians are very special, very amazing people. Previously I had considered them a clan apart, rather musty, stand-offish individuals, nursing superiority complexes. Now I appreciate them as real individuals. Sometimes they're characters, but they are wonderful ones, intelligent ones, most helpful ones. They're always holding out the assisting mind and the right book to the seeking mind and the outstretched hand.

I am deeply indebted to Michael Kennedy, Director of

the Historical Society of Montana, and its Library and Charles M. Russell Gallery, at Helena, Montana. Mr. Kennedy, himself a well-known author and editor, has assisted many a writer of western books to success. The library is not only a bulging treasure of western lore but its chief librarian, Miss Mary K. Dempsey, an attractive woman of great intelligence and great awareness, over the years helped me "pan the gold-dust" for my book and inspired me to "keep digging." Her patience, her time, her energy and ingenuity never wore thin.

Likewise my deepest appreciation to Mr. Vigilante, wherever he is, for starting me on the trail of *Vigilante Woman,* for his original suggestion that I write such a book.

I'm also most sincerely grateful to the following libraries for their assistance:

The Great Falls, Montana, Public Library, where I spent many fruitful hours in the large and well-ordered Western Room. There Mrs. Alma Jacobs, the librarian, nationally known in library circles, cheerfully and efficiently gave me invaluable help in my research work.

The Utah State Historical Library in Salt Lake City, Utah, where the talented and highly capable librarian, Mr. John James, assisted me. He followed the trail of each piece of western lore as assiduously as an FBI agent would a long-sought-after bank robber.

Also, my warm thanks to the Public Libraries in Butte, Helena, and Miles City, Montana; in San Francisco, Hayward and Ukiah, California; Reno, Nevada; Seattle and Spokane, Washington.

My eternal thanks to dear Courtenay for urging me to write this book and for the many valuable notes on the

Vigilante period which he bequeathed to me at the time of his death.

My sincere gratitude to Niven Busch, of Hollister, California, movie playwright (*Duel in the Sun, The Furies, The Actor*) and best-selling author (*The Hate Merchant, Day of the Conquerors, Twenty-One Americans, The Carrington Incident, They Dream of Home, California Street,* and *The San Franciscans*) for suggestions he gave me for the outline of *Vigilante Woman,* and his oft-expressed confidence that "I could do it—write the book."

My enduring thanks to the late Joseph Kinsey Howard, Great Falls, Montana, noted writer of Montana lore (*Montana, High, Wide, and Handsome, Montana Margins*) for research advice he gave me.

To John K. Hutchens, a native Montanan, now of Rye, New York, for many years a widely known book critic of New York newspapers, and now a member of the Board of Directors of The Book-of-the-Month Club, and himself a well-known author, for his inspirational help and his suggestions on writing and marketing the book.

To the late Ben Danforth, of Great Falls, Montana, who gave me the use of his huge and valuable library stocked with western Americana, especially that part relating to the Treasure State history, and for the knowledge of this region that he so generously shared with me.

To my brother, the late Frank A. Rowe, of Boulder, Montana, prominent mining man, whose adopted state was Montana, and who dug up many leads of valuable source material for me, who introduced me to several descendants of the Montana Vigilantes, who in turn gave me a rich bounty of background material. Also, to dear Frank, my always-present gratitude for the times he fed and housed me at his Comet mine cabin while I worked on *Vigilante Woman.*

My never-ceasing thanks to my husband, W. H. Towle, for driving me thousands of miles to do research work, without which freely given aid I could not have completed this book.

My oft-expressed appreciation to my daughter, Miss Dorothy Dunbar, herself an author (*Blood in the Parlor*), for the source material she unearthed for me, and for the practical aid she gave me in typing. Likewise her confidence and belief that "I could do it."

My gratitude to the old-timers who gave generously of their time and inherited information concerning the Montana Vigilantes. These include:

Lloyd Brooks, of Virginia City, Montana, former sheriff of Madison County; Miss Sarah Trout, formerly curator of the Virginia City, Montana, Museum, and descendant of Henry Gilbert, of Virginia City, who had the first brewery in Montana, establishing it in the Vigilante era in Virginia City; and the descendants of Charley Brown, one of the Montana Vigilantes.

Contents

Illustrations

Introduction

In the following pages we have written of the lives and loves of seven stout-hearted women who resided either in Virginia City or Bannack, Montana, during the stern— and necessary—reign of the Montana Vigilantes, a group of men who in 44 days hanged 25 road agents plus the peace-disturber "Cap'n" J. A. Slade. There were supposed to be 50 of these Vigilantes, who, indeed, were well dubbed as the "Fifty Righteous Hangmen."

Generally the Vigilante woman, the petticoated female behind this turbulent scene of 1863–1864, has gone unheralded and unsung. A woman of that era was in the news only three times: when she was born, when she was married, and when she died, or, as one pioneer woman tersely put it, "hatched, matched, and dispatched."

I do not attempt to present here just good and bad women. I do not even take a whirl at the futile task of painting a definite, single dimensional portrait of a Vigilante woman. They didn't all have painted faces under a hat heavily laden with swaying willow plumes. They didn't all wear faded sunbonnets, their faces leathery and pale. They weren't all narrow-minded, critical shrews, and neither were they all loose ladies with hands ever outstretched eagerly for the bulging poke of gold dust.

The Vigilante woman is therefore a composite picture. But no matter what the shadows and the highlights of that painting, it must, if authentic, reveal the quiet courage, the cool daring, the stout heart, the resourcefulness, and the undaunted, undiminishing bravery of this frontier woman. You cannot fairly put the imprint of "bad" on any one woman who remained steadfast to her man, a woman who had a code of honesty and wore a badge of courage as surely as she wore paint on her face or lace flounces on her sweeping skirts.

For there is one thing that never goes out of fashion: bravery!

Thus, we salute the bravery of the Vigilante woman, whether virtuous or a vixen. I can hope you like every one of them: the unforgettable, indomitable Mrs. Collins; the audacious, loyal Mrs. Slade; the Robin Hood of the frontier women, Madame Eleanore Dumont, whose flashing life came to such a dreary, sordid close; the pretty Lucia Darling Park, with her eager spirit of adventure ever stirring under a demure façade; the sorely tried but sincerely true—true to her principles—Electa Bryan Plummer; the dauntless and steadfast yet very understanding Harriett Sanders; the retiring Nettie Dimsdale (Foster), so overshadowed by her highly publicized husband, Thomas J. Dimsdale, as to be almost ignored historically.

The Bravest are the tenderest,
The loving are the daring!—Bayard Taylor

Vigilante Woman

1. Prologue:

Sob Sisters of Virginia City

It is ironic that the prologue to the saga of the Montana Vigilantes was written by the respectable women of Virginia City, Montana, whose usually rigid, straight-laced attitudes toward justice were shaken to maudlin sentimentality on June 29, 1863; ironic because the epilogue to this swift-moving, death-dealing drama was staged, ruthlessly and relentlessly, by the same good women on March 10, 1864.

During these nine turbulent months of robberies, stagecoach hold-ups, murders, and reckless lawlessness, Virginia City's respectable women underwent a change of heart that transformed their tender emotions into an aroused anger against any display of lawlessness, be it murder or drunken carousing and destruction of property. It was understandable, this right-about-face, this steely relentlessness of the good women, because during those stormy nine months their tolerance had been battered fiercely by a virtual reign of terror in the Alder Gulch and Grasshopper gold diggings.

In June, 1863, Haze Lyons, Buck Stinson, and Charley Forbes murdered D. H. Dillingham, a deputy sheriff. Stinson was a crooked deputy, taking orders from the crooked sheriff, Henry Plummer, while Lyons and Forbes were two of Plummer's murdering henchmen.

On June 28, 1863, Lyons and Stinson were found guilty of Dillingham's murder while Forbes was given a separate trial and acquitted. Immediately after the two men were condemned to hang for the crime, Judge William L. Steele ordered John X. Beidler and Richard Todd to erect a gallows and dig graves for Lyons and Stinson, who would be lodged in jail overnight while the preparations were completed for their demise.

The execution day dawned bright and clean. The sun was warm, the water of the nearby creek splashed cheerily over the stones of its bed, the sun-touched mountains reached majestically skyward, encircling the sprawling gulch-town, but no man—or woman, for that matter—had eyes for the brilliant June day. In fact, June made a futile attempt to attract the throng. Its glories passed unnoticed as the wagon bearing the condemned men jolted down the rutted-street from the log cabin jail to the gallows.

News of the proposed hanging resulted in a rush to the Gulch. Miners left their rockers, long toms, and sluice boxes. Housewives hurried from their homes. Courtesans ventured to the edge of the throng. Hurdy-gurdy girls huddled in a silent group.

A deep silence fell over the crowd that followed the tumbrel. The wagon finally hit a big rock in the bumpy road and from Haze Lyons' throat broke a gasping, tearing sob that ripped wide the silence of hundreds watching the progress of the death wagon. A woman—a good woman, too—morbidly gazing down from the hillside, echoed the terrible cry. "Oh, don't hang the poor boys," she screamed hysterically. "Don't hang them."

Other women, their nerves at a high, explosive tension, needed only this one woman's cry to unleash their compassionate, sentimental emotions, and they took up the plea. "Save them," they cried shrilly. "Save the poor boys' lives."

A friend of the doomed men leaped on the wagon and loudly demanded that he be allowed to read a farewell letter which he claimed Lyons had written to his old mother. Beidler, Todd, and the guards, hemmed in by the hysterical, female mob, now re-enforced by male friends of the convicted men, could do nothing but halt the wagon.

Slowly, passionately, effectively, the letter was read. It was warm with assurances of the boy's love for his mother, with sorrow for a crime into which he claimed he had been forced by evil associates, and with glowing pictures of the virtuously repentant life that would be his if only he could be granted another opportunity to go straight and redeem himself in the eyes of his fellow men.

The word "sob sister," with all the viciously maudlin sentimentality it implies, was yet to appear in the English language, but the sob sisters of Virginia City carried the day. And they were duped, too, as many sob sisters have been in subsequent years, and many more sob sisters will be fooled for centuries to come, or as long as villains are appealing and handsome and women have tender hearts.

They were duped because it was a matter of record that Haze Lyons never saw that tear-jerking letter to his mother; his friends, some of them educated and handy with words and pen, had written it.

"Give him a horse and let him go to his mother," came

the cry from the surging mob, the shrill sopranos floating high over the crowd.

"A vote. Let's have another vote. All in favor of turning them loose say 'Aye,' " yelled the chorus of both male and female voices.

A thundering answer of "No's" and "Ayes" (about equally divided) was the response.

Haze Lyons wept loudly; the women sobbed unrestrainedly. These women, it must be remembered, were the respectable wives and mothers of the town, not the hurdygurdy girls, the courtesans, the sweethearts of the road agents.

Finally, someone suggested that those in favor of hanging walk up the hill, and those for liberation of the men walk in the opposite direction. This method was not approved —in fact, some of the men felt it took too much effort to puff up the hill. One fat man yelled: "What the hell's the use of walking up a hill?"

At last, four men were selected and two were posted on each side of the crowd. Those in favor of the hanging were to walk between one pair, those against to march between the other couple.

The "Liberty Party" won by the simple expedient of the same men and women marching several times by the checkers keeping track of those voting in favor of turning the boys loose.

Deputy Sheriff Jack Gallagher—another of Plummer's road agents who himself was later to hang for his crimes— leaped to the wagon wheel beside the bound men, his cocked pistol gleaming in his hand, and roared gleefully, "They're cleared! Let them go!"

"Let them go! Let the poor boys go!" shrieked the misguided women.

Someone slashed the lariat that picketed a horse nearby, a horse belonging to a Blackfoot woman, and Stinson and Lyons leaped to the animal's back, kicked him lustily in the ribs, and galloped down the gulch—to freedom!

Judge Steele, the doctor-judge, was standing in the doorway of his cabin as the men passed on the Indian pony.

"Good-bye, Doc," the liberated murderers shouted to the astonishment of the jurist.

Behind the scoundrels, who would as soon have shot a good man down or slit his throat as flip a poker chip, the crowd scattered rapidly, the men supporters to drink toasts to their friends who had escaped death and to generally whoop it up in the saloons, the respectable women to discuss their victory over backyard fences or on the dusty main streets.

During all this noisy commotion, the poor victim, Dillingham, lay stark and stiff on a gambling table in a brush wickiup in the gulch. Soon a few men with more respect in their hearts than thirst in their throats gathered together, built a coffin, and laid the dead deputy away. One man, making a gesture of disgust, pointed to the unused gallows and exclaimed bitterly, "There's a monument to disappointed justice."

"The tears of my wife and daughter helped to save those poor boys from being hung," said a man named Burton.

Beidler turned on the speaker savagely and snapped, "I notice that they don't seem to have any tears for the man the poor boys murdered."

One woman who had clamored the loudest for the murderers' liberation was the very "good" woman who had put a sheet over the dead body of the slain, honest deputy sheriff, Dillingham. She justified her actions in asking that

Lyons and Stinson be freed on the grounds that she had seen Charley Forbes kill Dillingham, and that Lyons and Stinson were being hanged only to appease popular demand. She said her fight for the condemned men's lives was in the cause of fair play. Likewise, in leading her crusade for the murderers' freedom, she told the women that Charley Forbes was acquitted "because he was so handsome and so smart."

Thus, the hanging of Lyons was delayed six months by the vote of these respectable townswomen. But there's another view of the result of the sob sisters' sentimental spree; perhaps it crystallized action toward the definite formation of the Montana Vigilantes Committee. Maybe the episode hastened the advent of the Vigilantes, and proved that justice had to be unemotional, clear-headed, and stern if lawlessness was to be abolished in the West!

Professor Thomas J. Dimsdale, no doubt the most knowledgable chronicler of these early days, in his book *The Vigilantes of Montana,* first published in 1866, comments as follows on the drama put on by the ladies of Virginia City to insure reversal of the guilty verdict for the two condemned murderers:

We cannot blame the gentle-hearted creatures but we can deprecate the practice of admitting ladies to such places. They are out of their path. Such sights are unfit for them to behold, and in rough and masculine business of every kind women should bear no part. It unsexes them, and destroys the most lovely parts of their character. A woman is a queen in her own home; but we neither want her as a blacksmith, a ploughwoman, a soldier, a lawyer, a doctor, nor in any such professions or handicraft. As sisters, mothers, nurses, friends, sweethearts and wives, they are the salt of the earth, the sheet anchor of society, and the humanizing and purifying element of humanity. As such, they cannot be too much respected, loved, and protected. From Blue Stockings, Bloomers, and strong-minded she-males generally, "Good Lord, deliver us."

Next morning as the soft morning light stole over the Madison Divide, two dead bear cubs dangled at the end of the ropes on the cheated gallows and below them was a crudely lettered sign nailed to the gallows post, which read:

Two Graves for Rent

Apply to

X. Beidler

This unfortunate victory of Virginia City womenfolk in freeing the two murderers set back the reign of stern justice in Montana Territory for several months. But intervening events between this tender spring day and the grim winter executions of the murdering road agents turned the respectable women into relentless judges who demanded the execution of Captain Joseph A. Slade, who never killed a man in Montana.

"Oh, woman, thy name is inconsistency."

But the story of the Virginia City women who dealt the death blow to Slade is the epilogue of the Virginia City and Bannack story of Vigilante women.

2. Electa Bryan Plummer:

A Good Woman Who Loved a Bad Man

Mrs. Henry Plummer, nee Electa Bryan, a bride of less than four months, had a headache. She tossed and turned sleeplessly in the small, dark bedroom of the Plummers' honeymoon log cabin. It was late and she fretted because her law-enforcement husband once again was spending the night out. Where was he? Why did she have this severe headache, and what should she do for the nagging pain? The questions went unanswered, buzzing around her head like so many annoying gnats.

Finally it was past midnight, almost one o'clock. She took a candle from the nearby bedside table, lit it, threw on a pink and white flower-sprigged challis robe over her white muslin nightdress and went to the kitchen for a headache powder.

She was shocked to hear the rumble of low voices coming from the back stoop. Her terror lessened when she recognized her husband's voice and an occasional suggestion seemingly from several of his "deputies." But when she heard what they were plotting, she stood motionless as if frozen to the rough wooden floor-boards of the tiny kitchen. Her teeth chattered; she shivered as if seized with a chill.

Sheriff Henry Plummer, the one and only lawman for hundreds of miles in Idaho Territory (now Montana, Idaho, and Wyoming), and his henchmen were planning a stage holdup, which Electa knew, from hearing daily reports of such crimes, meant murder, too! She decided to leave her husband, then and there.

Electa no doubt recognized the voices of several of the men, matching voices to names, because Plummer frequently entertained his "deputies" or close friends at the newlyweds' cabin.

Plummer himself was as rare a character as American criminal history has produced, and not the least of his qualities was an appreciation of the unusual in other men. In George Ives he had one of the most striking and implausible characters that ever plundered and murdered on the western frontier. Ives was no commonplace frontier hoodlum, but engaging and quickwitted, fair-haired and well-dressed. In Boone Helm, Plummer had a killer whose ferocity, coupled with his self-proclaimed cannibalism, frightened even his fellow gangsters. Steve Marshland was a college graduate turned energetic road agent, but had the odd distinction of being averse to murder. "Deputy" Jack Gallagher, was the swaggering, bold, brazen type, the one Plummer sent out to do "glad-handing," with one hand for his genial duties, the other on his ever-ready gun.

Electa didn't know who all of Henry's midnight plotters were, but she knew with cold finality that her husband, her handsome, admired husband was up to no good.

The crushing, horrendous enormity of this midnight revelation concerning the man she adored made Electa forget even the purpose of her errand. The headache was ignored because the fresh pain, deeper and greater, one that would not yield to any mere physical medicine, was in her heart! Her idol not only had clay feet but the bloody hands of a killer.

After all these years, it's still a matter of debate whether Electa did know something about Henry and his murderous manipulations or whether she merely suspected that Henry was not the gentleman, the solid citizen, the fearless law enforcement officer that she believed him to be when she married him, and whether those plots she overheard in the kitchen for the first time revealed to her her husband's shocking duality. Some chroniclers contend that Electa knew some of Henry's criminal past, believed that he really wished to be a "good man," and that in a heroic, noble mood, she felt his deep need of her—and so married him.

Echoes of many quarrels had floated over the threshold of the Plummer cabin and become subjects of Bannack gossip. These verbal fights had started a short month after their marriage. 'Twas said that Henry was "a street angel and a home devil," being very irritable and short-tempered at home but very affable to the townspeople. The quarrels could have been caused by Henry breaking his promise "to lead a new life" and Electa upbraiding him for his return to evil companions and evil ways. Or she may not have known about Henry's past life, and merely suspected that he was mixed up in scandalous doings. She might have accused him of these dark misdeeds, which could have led to their quarreling and to Electa's demand that he change his ways or she would leave him.

Regardless of what made Electa decide to leave Henry's encircling, affectionate arms, it was a swift and final decision. She had been expecting the arrival of her sister and brother-in-law, Mr. and Mrs. J. A. Vail, from Sun River. They were to make their home in Bannack and Electa knew it would be just a few days before they'd arrive. She was very fond of her sister, Virginia, and her decision must have been a desperate one to cause her to miss greeting the Vails.

Mr. and Mrs. Vail reached Bannack within a few days after Electa took the stagecoach for the East. They moved in with Sheriff Plummer, Mrs. Vail keeping house for him and Mr. Vail running a Bannack store. The Vails believed in their brother-in-law up to the very last, even as he dangled from the end of the hangman's rope. They believed in his gallantry, his honesty. What the revelations following Henry's hanging did to the Vails' loyalty no one knew but Electa Plummer, who later went to make her home with them in Vermillion, South Dakota. She never discussed her life with Plummer or the desperado himself. She seemed to long to forget those dark Idaho chapters of her past.

The story of Electa Plummer is the age-old one of a good woman's attraction to a worthless bounder. It's the story of a good woman being drawn to an evil, dashing man whose very evilness is part of his allure for her, although she is unconscious of this warped attraction and would deny it, as Electa Plummer no doubt would have denied it.

The last persons to actually see Electa as she left Montana—and this was one of those queer coincidences of fate —was a party of Bannack-bound travelers who encountered Mrs. Plummer's stagecoach at the crossing of the Snake

River in Southern Idaho. The northbound travelers were headed by Sidney Edgerton of Ohio, recently appointed Chief Justice of the Idaho Territory by President Lincoln; Wilbur Fisk Sanders, who was to prosecute Plummer and his road agents; and Lucia Darling, Montana's first schoolteacher, whom we shall meet again in this chronicle. The members of the Edgerton party described Mrs. Plummer as very quiet, composed, and attractive.

After Electa went East, Henry spoke pleasantly, wistfully of his wife, and said that "she was lonely for her parents, whom she had not seen for some time, and had just gone to Cedar Rapids, Iowa, for a visit with them." He convincingly explained that because of his many duties as sheriff he could not get away to accompany Electa on her trip, but he planned to visit Electa's folks later, and then he and his wife would return to Bannack together. Soon, however, unless questioned outright, the sheriff made no mention of his wife. He no longer referred to her continued absence. It was said that Henry gave Electa $10,000 in gold dust when she scurried swiftly out of his life. Whether this is true or false, research fails to reveal.

Mrs. Plummer's life was conventional and uneventful up to the time she met Henry. She had a good education, taught school, was raised and educated in the East, and came West to visit her sister. But what of Henry's turbulent life of crime? One cannot present a complete portrait of Electa Plummer without dredging up a bit of Henry's filthy past, a past that wound over a bloody trail through California, Washington, Oregon, and the entire Idaho Territory.

Plummer was probably the greatest organizational genius in the history of American crime until the prohibition era, and it is doubtful if any of the racket kings have topped him. In him were combined, to a superlative degree, three qualities which seldom are found together: skill in planning and direction, utter lack of moral scruple, and audacity. These were coupled with charm and personality.

His gang—spies, couriers, horse-wranglers, the men who committed the actual stick-ups, the strong-arm men, and his deputies—in his road agent-sheriff days numbered not more than 30. Yet they had killed, by conservative estimates, some 300 gold-laden travellers from the Montana camps, and their loot must have been upwards of three or four million dollars by present-day values.

Plummer was the smooth gentleman-crook who never had a callous on his hands, never did any real work, but lived by his wits. The motto that guided his deviltry, and no doubt made him successful as a "high executive" of the road agents, was simple but direct and brutal: "It's quicker and safer to kill a man for his gold than dig for it."

It was this actual and insatiable desire for gold that led Plummer on to his destruction. He went always to new "diggins," being uncanny in ascertaining just where the first thin trickle of dust and nuggets would strengthen into a rich steady stream, and where victorious prospectors, their pockets and valises bulging with gold dust, would head for the "outside."

Biographical notes on Plummer are scant, so it is best to say that the early background is hazy and fictional, much of it of his own fantastic fashioning. We are told that he was five feet eight inches, five feet ten, and just under six feet. He weighed 145 pounds, or maybe 165. He had medium brown hair, dark brown hair, hair as black as an Indian's. His eyes were a piercing light blue, a steely gray, and they were pale and lifeless.

Likewise he was born in London, in New London, Connecticut, in New England, in New York State, or in Wisconsin; he was the scion of a "good family," and a butcher's apprentice; he always wore notably fine clothes and fresh linen, yet he appeared at his wedding in a checked flannel shirt and a suit patched with buckskin. Furthermore, whether he used any aliases or not, he seems to have spelled his name "Plummer," "Plumber," and "Plumer."

Plummer purposely confused the truth about his origin, so it's most difficult to separate the plausible from the fantastic, and arrive at an accurate picture of the true man and his background. Even Dimsdale, writing so soon after the man had been hanged, was forced to admit: "The most contradictory accounts of his place of birth and the scene of his early days are afloat; upwards of twenty versions have been recommended to me, each claiming to be the only true one."

To such a master of duplicity and deception as Plummer, lying probably came more naturally than telling the truth. It seems quite likely that he even lied about his lying; he "revealed" to William H. Rheem, briefly a lawyer at Bannack and a member of the First Territorial Legislature, that he "told varying accounts of his birthplace and family to avoid giving pain to a most estimable New England family," and then went on to tell the jurist that he was born in London in 1830, was apprenticed to a butcher at the age of eleven, ran away to New York at twelve, and lived there for two years "by the wiles of a street Arab" until he shipped to the Sacramento gold fields. He also told Rheem that he was a butcher in Sacramento "when he went with a crowd to the Salmon River diggings."

Actually we come on our first legal record of Plummer in California in 1857, and he was a baker, not a butcher.

He was also a part-time pimp; the cause of the entry on the court records was murder—the first of which we know, the first of how many we shall never know. Records further reveal that in October 1858, Henry Plummer, baker, of Nevada, California, was placed on trial for murder of one Thomas Vedder, and his lawyers asked for a change of venue because they felt their client "could not receive a fair trial in Nevada County" since, it seems, there had been considerable discussion among the tax-payers eligible for jury duty as to whether Plummer shouldn't be lynched. From the 15 pages in the California Law Review of 1858, in which the case is reported, it appears that the citizens took a dim view of the propriety of reversing the so-called "unwritten law." Plummer had seduced Mrs. Vedder, and Vedder's objection was Plummer's motive for ambushing him in the doorway of the Vedder home and giving him both barrels of a shotgun.

The change of venue was never granted, and Plummer was tried, convicted of second-degree murder, and sentenced to San Quentin. He was only in prison two months when he was granted a new trial by the California Supreme Court. Again Plummer was found guilty of second-degree murder and was returned to San Quentin, but before the end of 1858 he was freed by Governor John P. Weller's pardon.

Before he murdered Vedder, Plummer had been cloaked in the respectability of public office, for he had been elected, either in 1856 or 1857, marshal of the city of Nevada. Then he was re-elected to the office and later received the nomination of the Democratic party for the assembly. But he ruined his chances for election by his lawless and wild demeanor; the Democrats threw him out and elected another man.

After his pardon, he returned to Nevada City and became a partner in the "Lafayette Bakery." Soon, however, he was in trouble again, getting in a fight with a man from San Juan in a house of ill-fame. Plummer struck the man heavy blows in the head with his pistol, and the victim is said to have died a year and a half later from these injuries.

Later Plummer went to Washoe and joined a gang of road agents. He was mixed up in various hold-ups, including an attack on the Wells and Fargo bullion express. Dimsdale tells us that Plummer "leveled his gun at the driver, but the barrel fell off the stock, the key being out, and the driver, lashing his horses into full speed, escaped."

Plummer was tried for this holdup and was acquitted; he again returned to Nevada City. His next "escapade"— all such escapades being serious and murderous—was when he killed a man named Ryder in a brothel. Plummer had been living with a young woman in this house of prostitution and Ryder kept a mistress in the same place. Plummer was arrested but, through bribery of the jailer, walked out of the Nevada County Jailhouse.

Next he took on as his partner in crime a desperado named Mayfield, who had stabbed one Sheriff Blackburn to death. In fact, the ever-plotting Plummer helped Mayfield escape from jail, and the two started for Oregon. To throw off their pursuers, Plummer sent word to the California papers that he and his comrade had been hanged in Washington Territory for the murder of two men there.

It is said that all Plummer accomplished in Walla Walla, Territory of Washington, was seduction of a married woman. He went to Idaho with a new "partner," a man named Talbert, alias Cherokee Bob, who was killed at Florence because he was mixed up in the seduction scandal pulled off by Plummer in Walla Walla. Then Plummer popped up in Lewiston (Idaho Territory) and his new pal was a man named Ridgley. The pair went on to the Orofino diggings, where Plummer and his party of desperadoes got off to a robust start by murdering a dance-hall saloon owner.

From Orofino, Plummer went to Montana, leading a double life as the sheriff and as the chief of the most bloodthirsty, gold-hungry gang of marauding murderers the western frontier ever knew. He engineered hundreds of crimes, married the very respectable, attractive Electa Bryan, and hob-nobbed with the so-called "gentry" of Bannack and Virginia City, and other good citizens of the gold-mining settlements of Montana Territory.

With probably at least 15 merciless murders to his account, he reached the end of his trail on January 10, 1864, on a scaffold, which he, as sheriff, had ordered constructed to hang some horse thieves.

Into Bannack on the night of January 10, had ridden John Lott, a well-known merchant and trader of Virginia City, accompanied by four grim men from Alder Gulch, with a warrant for Plummer, Stinson, Forbes (former clerk of the miners' court), and Reeves, the latter three being road agents working for Plummer.

The men from Virginia City, with fellow Vigilantes of Bannack, picketed every trail leading out of town, then hunted out their men. Not a gun was pulled either by the Vigilantes or the four bandits; Plummer was taken in his shirt sleeves in the home of his sister-in-law, Mrs. J. A. Vail, and went so quietly that she suspected nothing of the purpose of the half dozen men who asked him, quietly, "to come downtown with them."

But it was Plummer, the man who had killed recklessly and had no mercy for any of his victims, who broke down when the Vigilantes brought him through the snow to the scaffold of his own making. He got down on his knees, clasped the legs of his disgusted captors, pleaded, prayed, and finally broke down completely. His maudlin dramatics were futile, and at the last minute he regained some of his old bravado and composure, mounted the box under the scaffold-pole, and stood quietly as his hands and feet were tied.

A shake of his head and silence met his executioners' question as to whether he wanted to send any message to his wife, the only woman in his long list of female associates he had ever married, the bride who had left him a few brief months after marriage.

Speaking of Plummer, Mrs. Plassman, the noted Montana historian, dips into her fine memory for the following:

The best dressed man in Bannack and its greatest villain was Henry Plummer. Where he got his clothes is an unsolved problem. His overcoat was that of an artillery man, its cape being lined with red. Plummer was never in the artillery so far as I can learn, and such coats were not for sale. So unusual was it to see one of its kind that it attracted considerable attention, and at one time advertised who he was, although he wore a mask.

I never heard of but one dinner party and that was given by Henry Plummer, with my father and Colonel Sanders and their wives as the invited guests. It was given in the Vail's little log cabin on Yankee Flat. With the full knowledge that their host was a double-dyed murderer, the guests did not feel called upon to wear purple and fine linen. Whether Colonel Sanders carried a derringer and kept his hand on it during the meal, I cannot say.

Historian Dimsdale in his biographical piece on Plummer in (*The Vigilantes of Montana*) ends his sketch with this philosophical paragraph:

As one instance of the many little incidents that so often change a man's destiny, it should be related that when Plum-

mer sold out of the United States Bakery to Louis Dreifus, he
had plenty of money and started for San Francisco, intending
to return to the East. It is supposed that his infatuation for a
Mexican courtesan induced him to forego his design and return
to Nevada City. But for this trifling interruption, he might
never have seen Montana, or died a felon's death. The mission
of Delilah is generally the same, whether her abode is the vale
of Sorek or the Rocky Mountains.

It was in 1862 that Plummer had arrived at a government Indian agricultural agency on Sun River, 60 miles
from Fort Benton. The agency, which sought to teach farm-
ing to the Indians, was run by J. A. Vail, and at the time
of Plummer's arrival there was a pretty guest at the Vail
home, no other than Electa Bryan, of Cedar Rapids, Iowa,
Mrs. Vail's sister.

Plummer liked Electa's fluffy, light brown hair, her big
gray eyes full of candor and softness, her slender, lovely
figure. He decided he was going to marry her.

Electa at first ignored Plummer. The dapper, handsome
villain seemed to have no appeal for her. Perhaps the very
fact that Electa was not immediately charmed piqued Plummer and thus sharpened his interest in the girl. He was
accustomed to having all women gaze at him with adora-
tion, fall under his mesmerizing spell, and even pursue
him.

Plummer remained at the Vails for two months, but he
had a bit of trouble persuading Electa to marry him, for
she was a thoroughly respectable young woman. Plummer,
however, had a way of dealing with women—his dealings
had sometimes taken a commercial turn—and he was by
any standard a personable, well-spoken, and well-mannered
young man who wore well-tailored black broadcloth coats
over his pistol scabbards and white linen shirts with a
sailor-knotted black scarf tucked under his collar. He is also

usually described as wearing a close-cropped mustache where many men wore beards.

He had another spot of trouble marrying the desirable pretty Electa. He knew that Jack Cleveland, an old friend, wanted to marry Electa, and had proposed to her. Jack also posed a double-threat to Henry because he was the only person in the whole Idaho Territory, the only living being, who knew of Henry's murderous past.

But Plummer was persevering in all things, whether matrimony or murder, and when he left Sun River, Electa had promised to be his bride.

The next few months were busy ones for Henry. He built a honeymoon log cabin for his bride. Then, with his customary cool and calculating strategy, he managed to eliminate the acting sheriff, Hank Crawford, who got tired of Plummer's hired assassins trying to kill him and finally went home to Wisconsin. Plummer eased himself in as sheriff, much to the relish of his old friends, who thought it a huge joke that Plummer, a murderer and escaped convict, was *The Law* in all this wild country.

However, before getting himself the job of sheriff, Plummer shot Jack Cleveland. Jack wasn't armed when Plummer attacked him, so that made it easier and quicker for the demon sheriff to shoot his old friend in the back. Through delays and manipulations, Plummer was acquitted of Cleveland's murder, for it seemed some of Henry's lying friends came forward and swore they had heard Jack make threats against Henry.

So now Henry was all set to take the 200-mile horseback ride through the frontier wilderness to marry Electa. Yes sir, everything was ship-shape: the cabin was completed, furnished, and ready to receive his bride; he'd closed Jack Cleveland's mouth forever, thus silencing any stories Jack could have told of his past, and any sweet words he might whisper to Electa. He also could lay boastfully at his bride's feet his badge of respectability, for now he was the sheriff, the highest law officer in eastern Idaho Territory!

Thus it must have been in a confident, gay mood that Plummer arrived at Fort Benton on June 2, 1863, where he was met by Electa and the Vails. The foursome stayed at the fort for 18 days awaiting the arrival of a minister to marry them. During this period, Henry, Electa, the Vails, and some of their newly made friends went antelope hunting and also enjoyed a sight-seeing trip to the Great Falls on the Missouri.

Finally the engaged couple decided to wait no longer for the Rev. Mr. Reed, who was to have married them, and they were wed on June 20, 1863, by Father Joseph Menetry (also spelled Menetre), of the Society of Jesuits, at St. Peter's Mission.

Francis M. Thompson, who attended the ceremony, wrote the following report of the wedding:

The pretty bride was neatly gowned in a brown calico dress and was modest and unassuming in appearance. The dapper groom wore a blue cotton shirt and blue necktie. The best man was the tall and graceful Joseph Swift, Jr., who wore sheep's gray pants, foxed with buckskin, a pretty red and white sash, and a gray flannel shirt and under the necessity of wearing moccasins, both of which were made for the same feet. Being a leader in Blackfoot fashions, he wore no coat. Mrs. Vail, the bride's sister, was matron of honor.

Mr. Thompson explains that in the absence of any woman to act as bridesmaid, he tied a white handkerchief around his arm and served in this capacity.

The wedding breakfast was baked buffalo hump and corn bread. The couple borrowed a government ambulance (which resembled the later buckboard) drawn by four half-wild, plunging, bucking Indian ponies.

Did Plummer marry Electa because he was really in love with her or was he just using a good woman to bolster his newly acquired respectability? Whatever the reason, he did marry Electa. His dealings with women, previous to his courtship of and his marriage to Electa, had been shady and shoddy. He'd become involved with married women; taken money from prostitutes; loved and left dozens of other women, some good, some bad, all wildly in love with him.

Was Electa aware of Plummer's criminal background at the time of their marriage? Did her passionate love for him make her believe that his reformation was sincere? Did she nurse that ego that women of yesterday and today have set up as the greatest feminine disillusion and matrimonial snare of all ages—that she was the *one and only* woman who could reform Henry Plummer? Or had he convinced this sheltered schoolteacher, who possessed more naivete than understanding of men, that he had been unfairly treated, misjudged, hounded by the law?

Whatever transpired between Electa and Henry, one thing was certain: Henry Plummer was a supersalesman of the western frontier in the sixties. He sold himself to the town of Bannack, he sold himself to Electa and the Vails, to the "solid citizens" of Bannack, Virginia City, and all the other mining settlements in that vicinity. But finally his luck ran out; his days of sunny, successful "selling" ended as he flapped ingloriously at the end of a rope, minus even his bride to comfort him.

When the Plummers arrived in Bannack, after their Fort Benton wedding, Plummer presented a self-done portrait of a "good man." He announced at the bars, in the gambling and dance halls, and to groups of his friends on the street: "Things are different now. I'm married and have something to live for. I have an official position and want to prove that I can be a good man among good men."

If Electa had stayed with him, been more determined and positive in her attitude toward Henry and not allowed him to stifle her objections with warm kisses, would he have broken with the road agents and really reformed? Or would he have continued to try and deceive her and would she have been forced to suffer the ordeal of his hanging right there in Bannack where she had come as a happy bride? It's history that Plummer became more violent, more daring and bolder in his crimes after Electa abandoned him.

Perhaps no respectable woman had more wild stories printed about her than Electa Bryan Plummer. Writers for years have contended:

1. She returned to Montana and found a large sum of money that Plummer had hidden away.

2. She entered a convent where she remained until she died.

3. She had a posthumous son by Plummer.

All these stories are false, and a letter written July 1, 1930, by Mrs. Plummer's step-daughter, Mrs. John Slattery of Wakonda, South Dakota, to the Montana Historical Society puts the label of fake on the various tales told about Mrs. Plummer after she left Montana, and belies the statement that "Mrs. Plummer became a Montana myth . . . was never heard of after she left Bannack." The letter, now on file in the Montana State Historical Library, follows:

Mrs. Plummer left Bannack less than six months after her marriage to Plummer. Mr. and Mrs. J. A. Vail [she was Mrs. Plummer's sister] moved from Bannack to Vermillion, Dakota

Territory, and Mrs. Plummer made her home with them when she was not away teaching school.

On January 19, 1874, Mrs. Plummer married Mr. James Maxwell, and became a step-mother to me and my sister, Mrs. Ida Stafford. She was also the mother of Vernon and Clarence Maxwell. She died May 5, 1912, and is buried in Wakonda, South Dakota. She had no children by Plummer.

She [Mrs. Electa Bryan Plummer Maxwell] never returned to Montana after leaving there. She was a fine, noble woman and a kind, good mother who took the place of our own mother. [Mrs. Slattery thus refers to her sister and herself who had been left motherless when very young by the death of the first Mrs. Maxwell. They were just little girls when Mr. Maxwell married Electa Plummer, and she raised them as affectionately as she did her own two sons by Mr. Maxwell.]

Mr. Maxwell was a prosperous farmer, his ranch being near Wakonda, South Dakota, where Electa Maxwell is buried.

And thus Electa Bryan Plummer Maxwell remains a symbol of what happened to many a woman on the frontier wilderness in those early days. She went courageously ahead and built a new life on the shattered remains of the old unhappy existence. She became a useful, happy wife and mother, taking great joy in her home, her church, her community, her children . . . and a good man!

Sometimes these "women with a past" were hurdy-gurdy girls, who left that flamboyant, insecure life behind them with a deep sigh of relief when they married a respectable frontier merchant, doctor, miner, or rancher. Perhaps, like Mrs. Plummer, they were good women who, blinded by love or a crusading spirit to reform a scoundrel, made an unfortunate marriage. Maybe some were even scarlet women who longed for respectability, and when they got it lived their new life with a devoted righteousness. Adventuresses on the frontier, spurred on by the necessity of survival, seemed to know how to fashion new and substantial lives out of chaos, out of cruel experiences.

Whatever Plummer thought of the girl who married him and then made him "the man she left behind," he never revealed. He took any such opinion with him to his grave. Death forever silenced any words of praise or condemnation that might have crowded to his lips.

Salute Electa Bryan Plummer Maxwell, then, as a woman of monumental though quiet courage! She may have appeared "mousey" or "very reserved," or, as Francis Thompson described her, as a bride "modest and unassuming," but here was a woman who faced up to the sorrowful knowledge that her honeymoon cabin had become a heartbreak house and who abandoned forever an impossible situation. She was strong enough emotionally to tear herself away from the fascinating charmer, Plummer, and go ahead in Spartan fashion to establish a new life for herself in another area of the western frontier.

She did not shun a fresh future, seek refuge in seclusion, or live mournfully in the past. Rather, she held her head high, accepted a second challenge from the sturdy West, and went on to a fresh start, a new marriage and a useful, contented life. She carried on valiantly, her hopes singing like the indifferent birds about a ruined palace.

3. Libby Smith Collins:

The Cattle Queen of Montana

In the late fall of 1863, Libby Smith, still in her twenties, walked serene and undisturbed through the hubbub of crime, vice, noise, gaiety, and work of booming, roaring Virginia City, Montana. The town burst out in all directions with gold, greed, industry, and destructive confusion.

Everywhere was the spirit of not only get-rich-quick but also spend-it-quick. The men lived, loved, gambled, worked, and fought; they labored ceaselessly and industriously by day for a poke of gold dust which the majority of them spent eagerly and recklessly at night in the saloons, gambling dens, dance halls, and brothels. These were the men immortalized by Bret Harte.

Even Bill Fairweather, one of the discoverers of these rich "diggings," rode in drunken glee up and down Virginia City's main street, scattering nuggets to the children, or plumping a fat gold dust poke into the lap of the first dance hall girl who threw him a wink and a kiss. He declared that gold was meant to be spent and spend it he did. A few short years later, Bill, who had taken millions out of Alder Gulch, died penniless.

At the time Libby came to Virginia City there were

12,000 men, a scant 100 respectable women, and 300 children.

Libby, with her sandy hair, a gentle powdering of freckles on her straight, rather wide snub nose, and a cheery smile on her generous mouth, walked unafraid and hopeful down the unpaved streets and the newly-made paths of the lusty mining town with purpose and faith in her heart, a heart that was never faint. She was determined to wrest a living from the frontier, to nurse her sick brother back to health, and at the same time to cheer the sick and discouraged. Temptations seemed to melt away from her faster than the first indecisive snow-flakes.

Undaunted, she went her way, her face inscrutable whether she stood in the shadow of the mining camp's gallows or walked with eyes straight ahead when a carriage approached bearing a satin-clad, bejeweled, and painted loose lady of the town. Or whether she recognized a swaggering road agent with his guns and knives bulging under his coat as he approached her.

These road agents, black-hearted, fast-shooting highwaymen, who had no regard for such a fragile thing as life, murdered and plundered, terrorizing the entire territory. Daily accounts of stage holdups, robberies, and murders were the news morsels heard on the street. Around the corner in a dimly lit building, members of the newly-formed Vigilante Committee discussed ways and means of stopping lawlessness in Virginia and Nevada Cities, Bannack, and the surrounding mining camps, all glutted with gold and its attendant temptations. In the tepees, tents, huts, miners' hovels, and even brush wickiups, life, love, birth, death, greed, murder, and gambling marched relentlessly, tempestuously on.

And in contrast to all this tumult and shouting, Libby

Smith walked unmolested and unperturbed. No doubt she carried in her thoughts the oft-repeated words of her wise mother: "Libby, remember a lady can be a lady wherever she may be."

Libby Smith had been carrying heavy responsibilities since she was ten years old back in her hometown and birthplace, Rockford, Illinois. She had been conditioned to the rigors, risks, and toughness of Virginia City through such experiences as being held captive for six months by an Indian tribe; being attacked by a mountain lion; being shot in the leg by stray bullets as she passed a gambling tent in newly-founded Denver just as a gun fight started; making twelve round trips from the Missouri River to Rocky Mountain points as cook on the Overland freight, the only woman among 160 males; and getting lost for four days in the Badlands.

Little did penniless Libby Smith dream—in that cold desperate winter of 1863–1864—that in later years she would become an affluent, nationally famous woman, called proudly by some "The Cattle Queen of Montana," and affectionately by others "The Cowboy's Mother," an intrepid woman who could deliver a baby or brand a steer with equal efficiency.

But as Libby said of herself, speaking of those days when as a young girl she was living in a crude log hut in pioneer Denver: "To complain was never one of my traits of nature, neither was the expression 'Give up' included in my limited vocabulary and I struggled on, hoping ever that better times and more comforts would fall to our lot."

And, thus, through hardships, temptations, tough jobs, and tough mining camps, often doing a man's work, Libby, calm and tranquil, went from one challenging incident to an even more hazardous one, and to many frontiers, each one newer and wilder than her last dwelling place. It was her faith in God and the goodness of people, commingled with the wise counselling of her marvelous mother, that seemed to bring Libby through wild adventures and landed her, unharmed, on safe and solid ground. Sturdy, staunch, and highly resourceful Libby was always ready—and sometimes it seemed even cheerfully willing—to face new and more dangerous hazards.

In the fall of 1863, Libby and her brother completed their 12th round trip with the freighting line and settled in Virginia City. Libby was penniless and her brother, who had been stricken with brain fever soon after their arrival in Virginia City, was unable to work. Although the trip from Omaha to Virginia City had taken three and a half gruelling, perilous months during which time Libby had not only encountered hardships but cooked for the 160 male employees of the Overland freighting outfit, she merely took a deep breath, threw back her strong shoulders, and looked hopefully around for a cabin for herself and sick brother. She knew that after they were settled she must seek a means of earning her living.

She located a small low cabin made of charred pine logs, with just holes for a door and windows. Libby covered the earth floor with four medium-sized cowhides held in place by wooden pegs. A sheet-iron stove, a few tin dishes, a small box for a table, and a homemade candleholder were the furnishings. Libby never mentioned beds, so one concludes that the "beds" were buffalo robes spread on the floor, as was often the pioneer custom.

Her brother still owned his mule team that he'd used in the freighting outfit, so Libby rented the team to a man who hauled wood, thus getting her wood and a little cash for the team's services. Then she heard that a Virginia City tailor was going to his native England for a visit and she rented his sewing machine—it was the first and only sewing machine in the mining camp—for seven dollars a month, and let it be known that she "was taking in sewing." Thus, soon after her and her brother's arrival in Virginia City, Libby was "in business" . . . and a respectable, legitimate business, too, which in 1863 in Virginia City was an oddity for an unmarried woman.

Soon, in addition to sewing for the Virginia City residents, Libby was given a contract for making flour sacks at five cents each. She was a fast worker and could turn out 100 sacks in a day and evening. It would seem that with her income from the flour sack contract, her sewing for individuals, and her cooking and house-cleaning for the miners, she could have made it financially. But, because of the severe winter and deep snows, there was no freighting between Salt Lake City and Virginia City, and since these Montanans depended mainly on the Mormon settlement for their supplies, food prices soared. During that winter of 1863–1864 in Virginia City a hundred-pound sack of flour cost $110; potatoes were 60 cents a pound, or $36 a bushel; eggs, $2.00 a dozen; butter, $1.50 a pound.

Nor was Libby reimbursed for all her work, for she often took care of the sick or cleaned for the needy without any payment except their warm thanks and their deep gratitude, which meant much to this woman who never passed up the plea of a fellow human being. Soon she was a well-known, respected citizen of Virginia City.

When Libby Smith, later Mrs. Nathaniel Collins, the "Cattle Queen of Montana," was rich and famous, she no doubt enjoyed many lavish Christmases, but none could give her the same warm glow as the memory of that cold, blustery Christmas of 1863 in her one-room cabin in Virginia City.

Christmas morning, when she opened her cabin door and the snow whirled about her and the wind howled, she found a sack of flour (remember that flour cost $110 a sack) to which was attached a card that read: "Merry Christmas from the Miners in remembrance of your kind acts and cheerful words."

Libby Smith dwelt in the shadow of the gallows. The gallows, of course, in the early days of the Vigilantes was improvised, a rafter in an unfinished building. "Regulation" gallows were erected later. As Libby traversed the streets of the turbulent town she hugged to herself the security of knowing that a Vigilante Committee was being organized. Something was being done to protect the decent people. Speaking of the Virginia City of those lawless days, Mrs. Collins wrote in her book, *The Cattle Queen of Montana*, the following frank description:

One of the chief evils of those early days was the saloon; the other, absence of good female society. Women of easy virtue were always present in large numbers, habited in the most costly and attractive apparel, brazen-faced and bold, promenading the streets and receiving fabulous sums for their purchased favors. Public gambling houses are on every street, with open doors and loud music, and are resorted to in broad daylight by hundreds; and as a matter of course, these places furnish another fruitful source of crime, inasmuch as all quarrels are commonly decided on the spot by an appeal to brute force, the stab of a knife, the discharge of a revolver.

In fact, all the temptations to vice are present and on full display with money in abundance to secure the gratification of the ruling passion of the mountaineer—the desire for novelty and excitement.

The mountains may be said to bound the paradise of amiable and energetic women. There seems to be a law unwritten, but scarcely ever transgressed, which assigns to a virtuous and amiable woman, a power for good which she can never hope to obtain elsewhere.

In his wildest excitement, a mountaineer respects a woman

and anything like an insult offered to a lady would be resented by any bystanding miner. For the preservation of those sacred rights and customs and the maintenance of these, the Montana Vigilantes banded together.

No Carrie Nation was Libby Smith, but with a good example, rather than a hatchet, she wielded a mighty power for good in Virginia City.

In describing the "arms of the road agents," Mrs. Collins wrote: "The road agents usually wore a pair of revolvers, a large double barreled shot-gun with the barrels cut short, and one or more knives or daggers."

Reminiscing about road agent George Ives' attire—it is rumored, but without confirmation, that she saw Ives hanged, but it is certain that she was in Virginia City on that fateful day—she wrote: "Ives wore a neat suit of black with the addition of a soldier's overcoat in the winter. A white felt hat at all times constituted his headdress."

An outspoken quote from Mrs. Collins' book describes the aftermath of the Vigilante's stern regime in Virginia City and Bannack:

As if by magic, the face of society was changed within a few short weeks; for it was soon known that in tones that might not be disregarded, the voice of Justice had spoken. Holding in one hand the swift-descending and inevitable sword of retribution, and in the other the invisible, yet effective shield of protection, the Vigilantes warned the thief to steal no more, commanded the brawler to cease from strife, and struck from his nerveless grasp the weapon of the assassin.

Was the struggle a mild and fitful one? No; for it was not before more than 100 valuable lives had been pitilessly sacrificed and 24 miscreants had met a dog's doom as the reward of their crimes that the end came and the "reign of terror" in Montana was brought to a close.

The cost of life necessary to bring about this result was indeed a heavy one, and the necessity for the sacrifice a deplorable event; but the results which followed gave sufficient proof of effectiveness of the methods employed.

Late in the spring of 1864, Libby and her brother moved to Harris Gulch, another mining camp fifteen miles distant from Virginia City. Her brother had recovered from his illness and went to work in the mines while Libby took in boarders. Two of her boarders were the Lindsley Brothers, and daily she took their warm lunches to them at the mines, giving this service, too, to many other mine laborers.

One noontime Libby called at a mine where one of the Lindsley brothers was working alone and found him trapped by the avalanche of a caving bank with his mouth held in a pool of water. With her usual quick wits Libby opened up a drain for the water and made the injured man as comfortable as possible. Then she hopped on a horse and made the 15 miles to Virginia City in an hour. There she got a doctor to care for Lindsley and several men to rescue him. Lindsley's leg was broken and his back so badly injured that it paralyzed both his legs.

Libby nursed the injured man until he was strong enough to go home to St. Louis, and accompanied him on his homeward journey. They went several hundred miles by horse and wagon into the Utah Territory to Bear River, where they boarded a train, the first train Libby had ever seen. She returned home in the spring, going as far as Ogden by train and then by stagecoach to Bannack, Montana. The journey took 12 days.

Her brother had left for Denver to join his mother and brother there, so Libby was alone and on her own in Bannack. She confessed that she only broke down and cried two times in her life: when she found herself alone in Bannack on her return from St. Louis, and the time she lost a prize horse in Great Falls, Montana, while accompanying her first load of cattle from Montana to Chicago.

But evidently Libby wasted little time on self-pity, for

she soon found a job as housekeeper and nurse for a highly respected Bannack woman, and also did a bit of outside nursing. Shortly after her arrival in rough-and-tumble Bannack, she delivered an eight-pound baby. A few months later she went to work for a doctor in Helena, Montana, where gold had been discovered in Last Chance Gulch. In the winter she returned to Bannack to run the general hospital for a Bannack doctor, receiving a salary of $25 a week, which was considered "big pay" for a woman.

But let's leave Libby in Bannack, where she seems to be prosperous, safe, and happy, and scan her earlier colorful life, the life she lived before arriving in Montana, which comprised one crisis after another. And let it be noted that Libby Smith Collins always met a crisis half-way without any feminine flinching. Repeatedly in *Cattle Queen of Montana* she mentions "tiring of the quiet life," and seeking new adventures. Numerous times, however, circumstances gave her no choice; she was forced to meet harrowing challenges to survive. Necessity didn't just nudge her, it pushed her forcibly to attempt the seeming impossible —and she survived victoriously.

As a child in a family of ten, Libby was picked continuously to do the toughest, most perilous errands. Writing of her childhood, she described herself as the "family roustabout," but added:

Had I been compelled to lead an indolent, hum-drum life, I should have been the most unhappy person on earth. This fact I can now realize more fully than ever before for I am now not only sunburnt by the glare of life but weather-beaten by its blasts.

Libby's family left Rockford, Illinois, for Iowa when she was ten years old, but she was a very mature ten-year-old child. There they settled in what is now Madison, Iowa, and lived in a log cabin. Later they crossed the plains to

Pike's Peak. Papa Smith, it appears, also had a keen, seemingly unappeased taste for new lands, new ventures, new sights. This same longing was to be his legacy to his daughter!

Libby was the only young girl in this party of more than 100 wagons headed for Pike's Peak. Even at that early date, she was quick of wit. A boy named Johnny, who was around fifteen, fell in love with this active, freckle-faced little girl, and followed her everywhere, which greatly irked her. Finally, one day, to his delight and amazement, she asked him to sit down beside her on the grass and visit. First, however, she spread her full skirt over a prickly-pear plant and then, politely, even cordially, urged the youthful, love-lorn swain to sit on her skirt. He did, with resultant howls of pain. Johnny did not bother Libby for the remainder of the trip.

It was on this trek that Libby first encountered an Indian chief's son who was later to recross her path and almost cost her her life, an experience that was to cast a long and frightening shadow on her future. Libby and some other members of the Pike's Peak party one day made a visit to an Indian burial ground. On the return from this jaunt, late in the afternoon, Libby was standing at the rear of the Smith's covered wagon, cooking their dinner, when the chief's son stole silently up behind her, grasped her tightly in his arms, and kissed her. Wham! Bang! Libby slapped his face so hard that the young Indian's nose bled profusely.

There was high excitement and worry in the camp, but the Indian chief, the kissing lad's father, saved the day by treating the incident as a joke. Mrs. Collins, years later, reported the kissing-slapping episode in her book: "As admiration for my courage, the chief presented me with a handsome pony."

At the end of six weeks the party reached what is now Denver. "Father decided to build a log cabin there," Mrs. Collins records in her memoirs. "I helped Father cut and haul the logs." The then youthful Libby, large and strong for her age, also rode the oxen as she and her father forded the river with the logs. It took Libby and her father eight days to haul the seven logs. The house when completed was 18 by 24 feet and had two windows which cost $1.00 apiece. Since lumber was $1.00 a foot, only half the floor in the cabin was covered.

By now money had run low, so Libby's mother, whose resourcefulness never reached ebb tide, took in boarders. Her cookstove was a campfire, her table a large stump. She charged $16 a week for meals.

The winter, according to Libby's reminiscences, was long, dreary and discouraging. Mrs. Smith came down with mountain fever and was moved to a neighbor's cabin, which was warmer, larger, and generally more comfortable. But the older woman's heavy duties fell on Libby's youthful shoulders and the young girl did the housework, washing, and cooking. The cooking for the boarders was all done over the fireplace. She burned her hands and blistered her face working at this chore.

One day a sick man called at the Smith cabin and told a glowing, alluring tale of gold being found in massive amounts in New Mexico. As a result of this tale, a company of 200 men, including Libby's father, was formed in May —a year after the Smith's arrival in Denver—and left for New Mexico. It was an ill-fated, futile trip, but, as usual, anywhere you found young Libby you found excitement aplenty.

It was on this trip that Libby was chased by a mountain lion, which measured six feet from tip to tip. Libby en-

countered the beast while she was out picking huckle-
berries some distance from where the prospectors had made
camp for the night. Libby took swift refuge in a tree and
stayed there until evening, as the lion lurked close by,
finally being rescued when members of the gold-seeking
party heard her screams.

At last the weary party arrived at the so-called gold fields
near Fort Pueblo and started prospecting. When no gold
showed up, members of the party became impatient, and
threatened to kill the man who had stopped at the Smith's
cabin in Denver and told the fabulous stories of gold existing in abundance in the Pueblo area. Kit Carson, the noted
western scout, chanced along at this time and visited the
camp. He showed the would-be miners nuggets he'd received from the Indians in this vicinity, and thus saved the
story-teller's life, much to the relief of the youthful Libby.
She felt sorry for the pitiful "prophet."

Slightly mollified, the company of 200 decided to divide,
with part of the group remaining near Pueblo and the
other half moving around the foot of the mountain to the
opposite side of the range. Libby's family remained in the
already established camp.

Then came another crisis: Libby's father took very ill
and she was selected to go around the mountain to the opposite camp for medicine. On the way she eluded a mountain lion, but just as Libby approached the opposite camp,
her destination, along came a temperamental jaguar and
her cubs. A man in that camp who came to Libby's rescue
was overpowered by the fierce animal, and as he fell his
gun flew out of his hands. Libby grabbed the gun and took
aim. Her first shot went into the man's thigh, and then she
aimed more slowly, more carefully, and killed the snarling
beast. She stayed long enough to care for the wounded man

and then hurried back to her camp with the medicine for her father. "Until his dying day, that man considered me the bravest woman on earth," chronicled Libby.

But there were also happy days for young Libby at this camp, for she made friends with the daughter of an Indian chief at an adjacent Indian village. The girls went riding and swimming together, and exchanged visits. The Indian maiden often gave Libby fine gifts, such as a handful of glittering rubies. These days of fun and pleasure, however, were short-lived because once again the prospectors became disgusted with dreary futile days of digging and the non-appearance of gold. Again their wrath came down on the party organizer and they decided to hang this man, whom they branded as a "teller of tales." This time there was no Kit Carson to save the unfortunate prospector, but until another rescuer came along twelve-year-old Libby was a strong substitute. Libby tells of saving the man's life:

As I knelt there begging for the life of that miserable man, there appeared to my aid an inspiration from the throne of God. My lips moved to utter words, savored with the intensity of human kindness, and as I spoke to them of the terrible act they were about to commit, their angry eyes flashed less brilliantly, their clenched fists relaxed, fell to their sides, shame spread its mantle over their flushed faces and they stood with bowed heads and gave heed to my entreaties, promising the while that the life of the man for whom I pleaded, should be spared.

The prospectors did, however, bind the man to a tree and switch him. Later the kind-hearted Libby took him food and water, also medicine to soothe his welts.

After spending six months in a vain search for gold, Libby and her family reutrned to Denver, which now was a well-established settlement. But once again tragedy dogged the girl's trail, for her father died in the spring and a few short months later, in the summer, a brother was murdered by the Indians.

In Denver, Libby encountered life "in the raw." She tells her readers that Denver was "real tough" at that time, and recounts how one day when she was passing a tent where gambling and fighting were going on, she was hit in the leg by a stray bullet before she could flee the scene of the ruckus. Later she wrote: "Murderers, desperadoes and gamblers were almost daily being shot down. Carl Woods, a gambler and murderer, was pursued, overtaken and shot down almost at my feet as I was one day in the act of crossing the Ferry Street bridge."

About this time, the Indians in the vicinity of Denver became very hostile and a family of white settlers was murdered near Cherry Creek. A posse that went out to investigate brought back the mutilated bodies of a man, woman, and child. Wrote Libby: "And the sickening sight of those bodies as they lay in the main street of Denver upon an over-turned wagon box will haunt me to my dying day. The man had been scalped and his body torn limb from limb —ears and nose had been chopped from his head." The woman's body had not only been mutilated but also ravished.

At that time the First Company of Denver Volunteers was organized with Colonel Chivington, presiding elder of the Methodist Church, as commander. Libby's brother was a member of this Company.

Later, when Libby's brother went prospecting, Libby and her mother moved to Central City, 25 miles from Denver, where they remained from late summer to the following spring. The brother returned because his hands and feet had been frozen. The mother came down with a severe attack of erysipelas, and the Smith family had run out of money. Libby, the intrepid teen-ager, as usual came to the rescue. She cared for two motherless children, for which the father paid her $40 a month, and that's what the Smiths lived on.

Soon the mother and brother took off for Iowa, the mother to sell the Smith farm there and the brother to marry his childhood sweetheart. Libby stayed in Denver to care for the two motherless children, as there was no money to pay for her trip. It was during this period that she learned the trade of glove-making. She received $10 for a pair of embroidered buckskin gloves. (Later a gift of a pair of these gloves saved her life and that of her fellow-travelers when they were lost in the Badlands.)

One evening, about twilight, she was out walking with her charges on the mountainside when she met a man and a woman, who from their loving conversation appeared to be sweethearts. Then, a little farther on, she met a man walking in the direction of the couple she'd passed. Soon came the sharp report of a gun. Libby retraced her steps and found the woman's escort dead from a gunshot wound. She reported the killing to the law authorities in Denver and the woman and the man with the gun were captured. Of this Libby wrote:

> The beautiful woman had, with fond words and tender caresses, enticed the man, known to have a considerable amount of money on his person, to the lonely mountain road and there . . . the companion of her guilt with his brutal hand and fiendish heart, under the cover of the pretended right of an outraged husband to summarily deal out punishment to the seducer of his wife, foully murdered him. The next day witnessed the execution of the guilty pair. Such was life in Central City at that time.

When Libby's mother, her brother, and his bride returned to Central City from Iowa, evidently the finances

of the Smith family had improved, due to the sale of the
Iowa farm, so they decided to take a pleasure trip to Pike's
Peak. This turned out to be a sorry trip instead of a joyful
journey as the Smiths had planned, for they were attacked
by hostile Indians.

Libby's brother threw a pair of overalls at his sister and
told her to put them on quickly so the Indians would not
know she was a girl. If the red men had known Libby was
a girl they would have captured her, as all white women
automatically were taken captives by the Indians during
all attacks. Although Libby escaped capture by the Indians,
she was hit in the leg by a stray bullet. Her brother carried
her to a secluded cave that he had discovered earlier when
he was scouting for Indians, and there he nursed her until
it was safe for her to be moved to a mining camp, where
she remained until her leg was healed. Three men and
one woman, members of the ill-fated Smith's sight-seeing
party, were captured by the marauding Indians; all four
were scalped and killed.

When Libby returned to Denver she had brain fever and
battled death for months. Finally her mother suggested that
Libby would convalesce more rapidly in the Smith's old
home in Iowa. Her brother recently had taken a job freighting across the plains, and it was decided that she would
travel eastward with him. As later described by Libby, this
journey was "pregnant with peril and suffering." Again
what appeared to be a pleasure trip for Libby turned out
to be an almost fatal and horrendous experience.

Libby and her brother had traveled for several hundred
miles, when they were attacked by Indians. She saw her
brother knocked unconscious from his horse, and believed
he was killed. Her captors blindfolded her, placed her on
a pony in front of an Indian warrior, and thus she traveled

for a night and a day. Then, her blindfold was removed but her hands and feet remained bound.

Libby's heart almost stopped beating when she saw that her captor was the Indian chief whose son she had slapped years ago. And there was the son, too, his eyes flashing with hatred. Almost immediately she heard the tortured screams of a white woman, captured with her, who was being ravished by Indians. Then she was forced to look on as the Indians tomahawked to death the woman's ten-year-old girl.

But once again Libby was delivered by the old chief, who called her "White Lily" as he gave his tribe his most prized horse as the purchase price for Libby. He put her for safe-keeping in a tepee with his daughter. Libby was safe for a while, but later the chief was so taunted by his tribal members for keeping a white girl that he ordered her to walk beside his pony, leading it over the rough trails while she stumbled wearily by its side. New horrors, too, flashed before her youthful eyes daily. She saw the squaws beat out the brains of a white baby by dashing it against a tree. She witnessed a weird barbaric ritual, the Indians wildly circling a collection of newly-acquired scalps, scalps of murdered white men and women.

While Libby was forced to watch these terrible and revolting crimes, she never gave up fighting for her survival. She had, when captured, hidden some matches in the hem of her skirt, planning to eat the sulphuric bits and commit suicide if the Indians attacked her. Three weeks after her capture, the old chief took his tribe, of which Libby was now considered a member, to fight another tribe. The chief's son, with nothing but evil in his heart, called on Libby. Knowing the old chief was no longer in camp to protect her, Libby pulled the matches from the hem of her skirt, rubbed them in her palms until sparks and brilliant phosphorous fell from her hands. The chief's son fled in panic from the tepee. Other Indians came to see Libby conjure up this strange light, these sparkling spirits. Awed and frightened, they scurried back to their own wigwams. They were convinced—as Libby hoped they would be—that she possessed some magic, supernatural power.

Another ordeal for Libby occurred when she was forced to watch as a Mexican man was fastened to a tree and burned alive. When she tried to cover her eyes in an attempt to shut out this frightful sight, the Indians pinioned her arms to her sides and compelled her to view this cruel and nauseating crime. She also saw an Indian belonging to an enemy tribe beaten and clubbed to death as he was made to run the gauntlet, shortly before she herself was forced to make this "run for her life."

The gauntlet was formed by two lines of Indians armed with clubs and tomahawks. The victim was compelled to run down the human alleyway. As Libby ran the gauntlet, she spied the old chief and, grabbing at a slim chance for survival, she broke through the line and fled to the tribal leader. An avenging squaw, armed with a tomahawk, pursued Libby and, as the girl reached the old chief, hit her an almost fatal blow in the neck. Libby was knocked unconscious; she also had a severe wound in her neck. She lay half-dead in her tepee for days, and then for many weeks was sick with fever. In the meantime, the white woman who had been captured with Libby died, leaving Libby the only white prisoner of the tribe with the exception of the white woman's twelve-year-old son.

When Libby recovered from her long illness, she performed the "match-trick" before the old chief, dramatically proclaiming she was a good spirit, placing her one hand over her own heart and her other hand over the chief's heart and promising that no harm would be inflicted by her on the Indians. The chief immediately issued an order that no one was to harm the "White Lily" under penalty of death. She was presented with a handsome buckskin suit and a beautiful pony. She was also allowed the liberty of the camp, and always the chief's daughter walked protectively by her side.

While being held in the Indian camp, Libby witnessed the Sun Dance, which was full of self-torture, and the equally cruel rituals for the selection of Medicine Men. No doubt she was one of the few white women ever to see these ceremonial dances, which later, because of their brutality and savagery, were prohibited in many sections of the United States.

After six months of these dangers and terrors, Libby was rescued by U. S. soldiers. The officer in command cautioned Libby: "Be brave, cling to the chief as if you wanted to remain."

This Libby did, much to the delight of the chief and his followers. Libby's brother, whom she feared had been killed, had been unconscious only briefly after he had been knocked from his horse at the time of Libby's capture, and was a member of the soldier troop that freed Libby. This reunion with her brother, no doubt, was one of the most joyous moments of her life.

The family had moved from Denver to nearby Cherry Creek in Libby's absence and she joined them there. But again the chapter could be entitled "She Found No Peace," for she had only been home a short time when the floods hit Denver and Cherry Creek. The Smith's home was swept away. Libby herself would have been drowned had not a passing rider rescued her from the swirling waters. The

Smiths took up their abode in a tent, as did many of the flood victims.

Again the Smith funds were wiped out, their home was gone, and Libby, barely recovered from her ordeal at the Indian camp, was faced with what seemed to be the eternal question that guided her gallant life: "What do we do now?" Providentially, and in answer to Libby's prayers, a wagon master appeared as the rescuer. He hired Libby's brother and gave Libby a job as a cook on the Overland freight. Of this period she wrote: "And for many a long dreary week, month, and year thereafter, my home was the wide, far-reaching plains and my abode the canvas-covered wagon in a freighting train."

Libby made twelve long, tedious trips from the Missouri River to Rocky Mountain points. "The men," she wrote, "were rough, uneducated, and unrefined but not a word of an insulting nature did I receive."

During her work with the freighting company, Libby met Captain J. A. Slade, shortly after he had murdered Jules Reni. Both Reni and Slade worked for the Overland freight. In an argument, Jules tried to kill Slade, who was unarmed, wounding Slade severely. When Slade recovered, he tied Jules up and shot him to death. He cut off Jules' ears from the mutilated body and carried them as good luck tokens in his pocket. Years later he was hanged by the Vigilantes in Virginia City, and it was said that these ears were still in his pocket.

On these trips, Libby encountered sandstorms, cold winds, snow, and drenching rains. In the winter, she often awakened to find four inches of snow on her blankets. No sissy could stand these elements, and Libby Smith never whined, complained, or allowed bad weather to defeat her.

Near Omaha one day she saw a man hanged from two

wagon tongues which had been raised and joined at the top to form an impromptu and hurriedly constructed "gallows." A drunken card player had shot another card player. Within 24 hours the murderer had been hanged and he and his victim buried. Rough grave markers were hastily made. On one was printed: "Shot. He was innocent." On the other: "Hung. He was guilty."

Libby also witnessed fights aplenty. One of the most fiercely fought, yet amusing, was between a burly Irishman and a dignified-looking minister, with the minister winning the bout.

Indian scouts, of course, were part of the wagon train, and one day on the Little Blue River, 25 miles below Fort Carney, Libby saw a scout hit by an Indian arrow. As usual, the dauntless Libby, unmindful of her own danger, grabbed a pony and rode into the jaws of Death to save the scout. All the wagon train men yelled in vain for her to come back. She scooped up the wounded scout, put him on her pony, and brought the frightened animal to the station corral with arrows flying thick and fast all around her. Then came a fierce Indian attack and the Indians and the wagon train men fought for four days and four nights before soldiers arrived to reinforce the wagon train crews and defeat the Indians. The soldiers reported that another nearby wagon train had had a similar attack; every member of the train had been killed.

On Libby's last trip with the Overland freight, several of her party were killed by the Indians. The wagon train was divided at Crazy Woman's Fork and Libby was selected as leader of the scouts for her outfit. It was her duty to ride ahead of the train and scout for Indians. They reached Fort Smith on the Big Horn River safely.

Just a couple of weeks after passing Fort Smith, an Indian saved Libby's life. Indian hunters had wounded a buffalo bull and then surrounded him to make the kill. Libby approached the circle of Indian hunters to get a close-up view of the maneuvers. She was within 100 yards of the wounded bull when he suddenly sprang to his feet, broke through the circle of horsemen and, with lowered head, flashing eyes, and deep and thundering bellowings of rage, made straight for Libby. Libby thought fast and moved faster, gaining the frail safety of a small cottonwood tree behind which she hid, clinging to it with tense arms. The beast lunged by her, and then, doubly maddened by her evasion of him, started back for her. At that very moment an Indian swooped her up onto his pony. Again the buffalo turned and was almost upon them when the Indian with kicks and yells urged his pony at a terrific pace direct for the camp, reaching safety just as a dozen men with rifles in hand killed the enraged beast.

The Indians presented Libby with the bull's tongue, which was the greatest token of friendship they could bestow. The Indians were very curious about Libby, for she was the first white woman many of them had seen. She had to run away from them and stay hidden in camp; the Indians constantly wanted to touch and even pinch her.

The next adventure—or should we say misadventure— of Miss Libby Smith was when her train was lost in the Badlands. Libby had received a case of canned fruit from the commanding officer at Fort Reno in appreciation for a pair of buckskin gloves she had made for him. The juice from this canned fruit saved her and her companions' lives. For three days, all they had to drink was the juice, and it was necessary to use it in such small amounts that the wagon train members simply wet their lips with it.

There was no food, no water, the travelers were weakened by hunger, there were Indians to fear at all times, and howling wolves at night. After four days of this danger and suffering, they found water on the summit of the mountain at Clark's Fork. The train rested there for three days and then proceeded on through the country now known as Yellowstone National Park. Then it pushed on to the Gallatin Valley and Bozeman, the wagon arriving at Virginia City, Montana, in the fall of 1863.

It was in this Vigilante town that we first encountered Libby earlier in this chapter. From Virginia City she traveled to Bannack, and it was in Bannack that we left her, working as a nurse for $25 a week, and it is with a more complete understanding of her past that we now pick up the threads of her life from that point.

From Bannack Libby went to Helena, which was a prospering gold "diggings" grown into a real town and the third, and permanent, capital of Montana. Libby was doing very well there in a private nursing job when fire swept the town. That night she lost everything, even her patient.

Once again "our heroine" was penniless. While looking around for a job, she was called to Silver City, 12 miles from Helena, to care for a sick friend. The fire that took all her savings and possessions was in February, and by May the indomitable Libby had once again landed on her feet and had a job as cook for the Canyon Creek miners at $75 a month.

That Christmas of 1873 was a deeply romantic one in Libby's life, for when she went to Helena for the holidays, she and Nathaniel Collins, who had been her beau for two years, decided to get married. The wedding took place on New Year's Eve of 1874, the bride being thirty years old at that time. Libby was especially proud that on their honeymoon they bought a cow for $75 before returning to Silver City. It was quite an achievement to own a cow in those days, since hay was $20 to $30 a ton.

On November 19th, Mr. Collins fell and injured himself. Mrs. Collins went to the spring to get some water and slipped and shattered her ankle. She crawled back to the house on her hands and knees, making her way painfully up the slippery path. She and her husband lay there for two days and nights without food, heat, or medical help. Then a Chinaman named Old John arrived and brought aid to the injured pair. They were in a Helena hospital from November to May, and it cost them $1500! The night they arrived home in Silver City, the reservoir and sluice boxes were destroyed by terrific rains; the loss was $1,000.

The following August the Collinses sold their mine and bought a ranch in Prickly Pear Valley, eight miles from their former mining home in Silver City. They stocked it with 180 head of cattle. Later they settled at Old Agency, Choteau County, now Choteau in Teton County. A daughter was born to them in November 1881, the first white child to be born in Choteau. Libby lived for an entire year on the new ranch without seeing another white woman.

In 1886, the Collinses moved to Willow Creek, Teton County, 24 miles from Choteau. In the Chicago *Drovers' Journal* of October 1891, we find the following item: "Mrs. Nat Collins of Choteau, Montana, is here with cattle that sold at $3.65 to $4.00. Mrs. Collins enjoys the distinction of being the first lady cattle shipper from Montana to the Chicago market."

Prior to shipping the stock from Montana to Chicago, the Collinses sold their cattle through buyers who called at their ranch. Libby urged Nat to ship his cattle to Chicago, and he did, making more money that way. The second year, just at shipping time, Mr. Collins took ill and Mrs. Collins decided she would take the cattle to Chicago herself. She headed the cowboys, driving the cattle from Choteau to Great Falls, from which point they were shipped by train to Chicago. It took four days to get the cattle from Choteau to Great Falls.

At that time a woman was not allowed to accompany her stock to market. Mrs. Collins waited ten days and finally received special permission to ride with her cattle to market. She rode in the caboose of the cattle train. Dozens of cowboys—many of whom she had befriended—came to the train to give her a "send-off," waved their sombreros high in the air, and sang out: "Success to Aunty Collins, the Cattle Queen of Montana."

When she reached St. Paul, she was given a pass to travel to Chicago in a passenger train and arrived there ahead of the cattle. She went personally to the stockyards, disposed of her stock, and received a much larger sum of money for them than if she had sold to the cattle buyers who came to their ranch or had marketed them in Great Falls. The following item was printed in a Montana paper of that period:

Mrs. Nat Collins has earned for herself the distinction of being the first and only lady in Montana to raise, ship and accompany the train bearing her stock to the Chicago market and personally supervise the unloading of the animals and their sale, and throughout the length and breadth of the land she is known as "The Cattle Queen of Montana." She is well informed on every subject pertaining to stock raising and her judgment is often asked by others regarding purchases and other matters pertaining to the industry.

Personally, Mrs. Collins is a charming lady. There is nothing masculine in her appearance or conversation. Her home life is pleasant and her homes—for she divides her time between a town and country residence—are beautifully furnished. No one would suspect in engaging in conversation with this modest and unpretending lady, that she is the manager of a large stock business—a duty which devolves on her by reason of her husband's poor health. Her homes are decorated with many specimens of her handiwork. She is an artist of no mean pretensions and many a charming sketch and bit of coloring are the product of her brush.

Socially she is very highly esteemed by all who know her and in the financial and business centers, she commands universal admiration for her thorough knowledge on every subject of her affairs for "The Cattle Queen of Montana" is indeed a financier and has succeeded in accumulating a fortune. Mrs. Collins is, in fact, a lady of whom Montana may well be justly proud.

The ranch was making stacks of money for the Collinses. Mrs. Collins was being accorded much publicity and many honors because of her outstanding achievements, especially outstanding for a woman; she was still the only woman to take her stock to the Chicago market. She had two lovely homes. She could travel anywhere a travel pamphlet suggested or her desires dictated. Her family was devoted to her and she and her husband were most companionable.

But remember, this was the same woman who had spent six months among hostile, cruel Indians; the same person who had made twelve round trips on the Overland freight, the only woman ever employed on a freighting line; the very woman who arrived penniless in Virginia City, Montana, during the death-dealing Vigilante reign; the woman who had spent one whole year on her Choteau ranch without seeing a white woman, and who had given birth to the first white child in Teton County; the woman who had mined and been foreman and cook for a crew of 18 miners. . . .

This was no "rocking chair" lady. She was, to the very last, a "woman of action." So in the early nineties, she announced, "I'm tired of the quiet life," and went to Nome, Alaska, in search of gold and adventure—mostly adventure. This was one of the few failures Libby Smith Collins suffered, but when she returned there were no gripings, no recriminations. She resumed her cattle business enthusiastically, and continued to prosper.

Three years after her return from Nome, Mr. Collins died. In her sunset years, Mrs. Collins spent some time in California. In the early 1900's she lectured all over the United States, telling the nation of the beauties, the glories, the opportunities, the history of the West, especially of her beloved Montana.

For 16 years Mrs. Collins' ranch was surrounded, inhabited, populated by cowboys, many of whom she befriended. She listened to their troubles, cared for them when they were ill, "tided them over" when they were broke. Of her cowboys she wrote:

I am prepared to say that the Montana cowboy is a fair-minded, noble-hearted, generous and whole-souled man. Many are the poor boys whose broken arms and limbs I have bandaged as they lay upon rocks or dry hard earth of the prairie, far from home or habitation, where they had been injured by a vicious horse or enraged animal and in this manner I earned the title of "Aunty" or "Mother" and in the possession of such cognomens I cannot but feel exceeding pride, for I have learned to look upon these boys, now that I know them so well, as true types of manly courage, generosity, and activity.

I may be peculiar in my likes and dislikes—cranky in the opinion of the cod-fish aristocracy—but, nevertheless, I would rather today be the "Aunty" or "Mother" and "Cattle Queen of Montana" than sit upon the throne of a real queen.

Libby Smith Collins died in May 1921. But no one can deny that her spirit, that gallant, never wavering spirit, goes steadily marching on!

She was an extraordinary woman, who lived in the Vigilante days in Virginia City, but she had a broad sympathetic nature that made her understand the miner, the mountaineer, the cowboy, the Vigilantes themselves, and reach for the soft and good underneath the hard and rough exteriors.

4. Lucia Darling Park:

Courage and Determination Behind a Demure Façade

Teaching school in the far West in 1863–1870 was no job for a sissy, let alone a girl from the East who had been sheltered and reared behind a white picket fence.

Such a girl was Lucia Darling, of Tallmadge, Ohio, who crossed the plains to Bannack, Montana, in 1863. Lucia brought with her a burning, unquenchable desire to teach school in a log cabin. She also craved adventure—wanted to share in the excitement, dangers, challenges of this new country. She was endowed with a lively nature that reached out daringly for stirring experiences. But like all young ladies of her era she had been drilled consistently in "restraint," or, in other words, "to always be a lady." And ladies, it seemed, maintained a serenity even here on the western frontier, where guns popped and drunken men reeled along dusty paths, euphemistically called "streets."

As they say in the movie scripts:

We first meet our heroine as she walks down the main street of Bannack, Montana, then part of the Idaho Territory, in

October 1863. She wears a voluminous brown cape, a perky little brown bonnet—fashioned by the deft hands of a Tallmadge, Ohio, milliner—with a daring red rose on it, the bright flower seeming to apologize for her drab attire. White frills trim her demure brown dress at throat and wrists. The bodice of her dress is fitted; her skirt, which she tries to hold free of the dusty street, is long and full.

Lucia is skipping to keep up with her Uncle Sidney Edgerton, who takes big confident strides down the rutted, dusty street. He is very distinguished and confident-looking, bearing more visible stamps of the East than the West. You know at once he is no mining man. . . .

And the last phrase of the make-believe script was so right. Edgerton, a Tallmadge, Ohio, lawyer, had been appointed chief justice of the Idaho Territory by President Lincoln himself in the spring of 1863. Soon he was the first governor of the Territory of Montana. It had taken Edgerton, his family, and relatives three and a half months to cross the plains. They'd arrived in Bannack in September.

Every day since that time, determined, persistent Lucia, his niece, had begged him to find a schoolhouse so she could start teaching school. So they were on their way, this crisp October morning, to interview the owner of a cabin to be used as a schoolhouse. Her eyes danced with anticipation as she talked about the school. Her face seemed to glow and shine, for she had the kind of countenance that radiantly lit up any room she entered, even if it be a gloomy one and all the people in it dour.

On this October morning a cold, tingling wind from the mountains, which were still seered brown from the summer's blazing sun and hot withering breezes, swept down the rutted streets. The turbulent mining town lying in the hollow of the towering mountains fairly jumped with life. Saloons, gambling halls, hurdy-gurdy houses bulged with people. Down the streets rode men on horseback, some bent on legitimate, useful errands; others on murderous business, prompted by a so-called easy but actually cold, cruel method of obtaining gold dust. Gambling was proceeding feverishly, even sometimes frantically, in low and long log buildings and in tents. Saloons resounded from loud talk, music, and the frequent crack of a pistol. Painted women stumbled down the street, teetering on their high heels, determinedly set on obtaining a number of plump pokes of gold dust before twilight settled over the blaring gold camp.

There was lots of living, gambling, mining, killing, and illicit love going on in this ugly, brawling gold camp, but very little psalm singing and education. Education and religion were deferred blessings of these early mining camps. First, came the miners and then the dance hall girls. These two lusty contingents were swiftly followed by the saloon keepers and gamblers, the storekeepers, and then the robbing, thieving, murdering crooks such as the notorious, and at this time especially active, road agents of Bannack, Virginia, and Nevada Cities, and other adjacent gold mining settlements. Their leader, paradoxically, was none other than Sheriff Henry Plummer, whose home was in Bannack but who could be found anywhere there was a hefty shipment of gold. He headed a band of road agents, some thirty in number, who plotted, plundered and killed with a gory pride.

But on this morning of October 1863 in Bannack, we're not so concerned with the dudish, two-timing Sheriff Plummer as we are with this couple walking briskly up and down Bannack's main street—well, as briskly as the ruts and the crowd permitted.

When they reached the cabin, owned by one of the biggest landowners and richest men in Bannack, their knock was answered by a groaning "Come in."

The cabin's owner, a "landed gentleman," had an immense affinity for whiskey, so that when Judge Edgerton and niece Lucia stepped inside, they saw a bleary-eyed creature huddling in misery on the floor under his buffalo robes.

In her prim, schoolteacher parlance, Lucia described in her diary the owner of the cabin: "He was recovering from imbibing too freely from the favorite and profuse beverage then so plenty and his voice was still too thick to be easily understood." (What Lucia meant was that the gent had a colossal hang-over!)

Judge Edgerton explained their mission to the cabin owner, who agreed that there should be a school in Bannack, and, according to Lucia, he said: "Damned shame, children running around the streets; ought to be in school. I will do anything I can to help you; you can have this room. Cheap, too, real cheap. Only $50 a month."

Uncle Sidney and Lucia agreed that $50 was too much to pay for a small one-room cabin with a dirt floor, one door, one window, and a leaky roof. Thus they decided that Lucia should hold school in the Edgerton cabin where she made her home. It had five rooms and had formerly been used as a store. There were carpets on the floors and pictures on the muslin covered walls. Lucia described the dwelling as "comfortable and homelike" and then added: "When one has been moving for months, he is not inclined to be fastidious as to the style of home he occupies."

This remark was no doubt inspired by the still fresh memories of that three-and-a-half-month trek across the plains when Lucia had jolted over rough roads in a covered wagon, bathed in cold mountain streams, got her hands and face blistered cooking over open campfires and subduing a stubborn, smoking little sheet-metal camp stove. Then, too, there were those lonely night watches when with loaded revolver across her lap Lucia took her turn "on guard" to watch for wolves, bears, and hostile Indians.

So this house, fashioned out of an old store building, seemed almost palatial to the young Ohio girl who faced the West with high spirits rather than fear, terror, or homesickness.

Thus, with her demureness ever hiding a daring heart, Lucia started on her school duties, with big plans for her little pupils. The first schoolteacher of Montana was the possessor of an ever-bubbling spring of inspiration. She wasn't depressed by the fact that the schoolroom stood right in the shadow of the gallows, the very gallows on which Sheriff Henry Plummer was to swing to his doom in a few short months, or that her pupils lacked uniform textbooks. (These books came from many states, Maine to Michigan, and each volume was different, defying classification.)

Soon a small log cabin was built to house Montana's first public school. Floating out the windows of the crude little schoolhouse and over the top of the gallows went the children's high, sweet voices singing "A Southerly Wind and a Cloudy Sky," lead of course, by the strong, sure soprano voice of Lucia Darling.

Mrs. Martha Edgerton Plassman, Lucia's cousin and well-known Montana author and historian, wrote in 1904 of this first Montana School: "That queer, dear little schoolhouse—its pupils who are living and are now widely-scattered, all bear witness to the fact that they drew as much inspiration from the rare personality of their teacher as from their books."

Lucia describes her arrival in Bannack on September 17, 1863:

It was afternoon before we at last halted on Salt Lake Hill and looked down upon the little settlement along the banks of the Grasshopper. The view was not an inspiring one. There were a few log houses of somewhat diminuitive size on Yankee Flats and across the creek upon a bar that wound along the valley not far from the bank of the stream were log houses of varying sizes and descriptions.

In the distance, the most conspicuous sight was the gallows, fitly erected near the graveyard in Hangmen's Gulch, just beyond the town, and on which we were told Union men were hung. Of course, this was only a report but it was during the Civil War and much bitter feeling existed among the people, many of whom had fled to the mountains to avoid the troubles consequent thereon.

Granville Stuart, one of the intrepid founders of Montana, a gallant man who made a notable contribution to the written history of Montana in his two-volume offering *Forty Years on the Frontier,* writes of the Bannack of Lucia Darling's early days there, 1863–1865:

Murders, robberies, and shooting scrapes were of frequent occurrence. The rich diggins of Grasshopper Creek attracted many undesirable characters and I believe there were more desperadoes and lawless characters in Bannack in the winters of 1862, 1863 and 1864 than ever infested any other mining camp of its size. Murders, robberies, and shooting scrapes were of every day occurrence in daylight as well as at night.

Mr. Stuart further writes that in late 1862 and 1863 there were only 30 white women in Bannack, of whom seven were married. He wrote, of course, of the "good women," not including the scarlet ones in his statistics. He described the social life of the town:

We had a number of fine balls attended by all the respectable people and enjoyed by young and old alike. Best suits, packed in the bottom of our "war bags" and long-forgotten, were dragged out, aired and pressed as best we could and made ready for these festive occasions. A very few of the men, who had their wives with them, sported white shirts with stiffly starched bosoms, but the majority wore flannel shirts with soft collars and neckties. These dances were orderly; no man that

was drinking was allowed in the hall. There were usually about
ten men to every woman so the women danced every dance.
Tickets were $5.00 gold and no supper was served. Two fiddlers
furnished the dance music.

Mr. Stuart also informs us that in Bannack in 1863,
chewing tobacco sold for $15.00 a pound, and shovels were
$10.00 each.

Lucia herself, years later, wrote the following for the
Montana State Historical Society, concerning the early-day
Bannack:

There are unwritten chapters in the history of every new
settlement which no pen will ever write but could they be written they would tell of the many heroines as well as heroes,
women as brave and deserving of credit as those who landed
from the Mayflower. They had much to do in winning the West
and a higher civilization has always followed closely in the
footsteps of the women pioneers.

It is the pioneer homemaker and the pioneer schoolteacher
who has paved the way for the permanent church and Sunday
School and have often asserted a more lasting influence than
was realized at the time.

Bannack was tumultuous and rough and the headquarters of
the band of highwaymen, and lawlessness and misrule seemed
to be the prevailing spirit of the place.

But into this little town had drifted many worthy people who
unbendingly held firmly to their principles of right. There
were few families there and the parents were anxious to have
their children in schools and it never was known when there
came a cry from the children that some school ma'am did not
rise up in response.

The exciting time when the Vigilante Committee effectually
rid the territory of the band of highwaymen occurred during
this period and the gallows tree up Hangmen's Gulch many
times bore fruit for the healing of the nation—the school was
not pretentious but it was in response to the yearning for education and it was the *first*.

What was there for young Lucia to do in Bannack besides teaching school? Because of the roughness, toughness,

and general lawlessness of the town, especially in Lucia's first year there, before the road-agents' gang was eliminated, the respectable women of the town stayed very close to home. So Lucia sewed, read, sang, and visited with her young cousins. The men of the households did the shopping and marketing because one could never tell when a stray shot from a saloon or gambling hall brawl might zip through the air and claim some innocent victim. Also, daylight holdups on the crowded main street were not uncommon and attracted little notice.

Lucia no doubt attended a few of the territorial legislature's sessions, as Bannack was the first state capital. She may have, with her relatives and a few close friends, even danced or played games. The popular dances of that time were the schottische, polka, Virginia reel, and waltz. Euchre was the favorite card game in the homes of that day, but no mention is made of "ladies" playing cards in Bannack. Canned cove oysters, crackers, and coffee, all of which were highly expensive, were the favorite evening refreshments.

No guest list is available for the lavish dinner party hosted by Sheriff Henry Plummer a few weeks before he was hanged by the Vigilantes, but since Lucia's Aunt and Uncle, the Edgertons, and her cousins, the Sanderses, were guests, no doubt Lucia, too, was present at this virtual Belshazzar feast.

Yet there was never lack of exciting news in Lucia's new home, and it did not come from the East either. These daily alarming bulletins of boistering Bannack came via Uncle Sidney Edgerton and Cousin Wilbur Fisk Sanders. No doubt Lucia's sharp ears picked up the low-voiced exchange of news between Judge Edgerton and Mr. Sanders, for they had much to discuss in that grim, bloody winter of 1863–1864. Mr. Sanders was a member of the Executive

Committee of the Montana Vigilantes. (He was also to serve as prosecutor in the later murder trial of the accused road agents.) Judge Edgerton was vitally interested in seeing law and order established in this western country and gave the Vigilantes much wise guidance.

Lucia never discussed the hanging of Plummer or talked much of the wild depredations, the cold-blooded crimes of the road agents, but she was there. She saw the limp bodies of the murderers swinging from the gallows; she knew of the crimes committed daily in Montana. She worked and prayed for the progress of the schools and churches, and lived to see both holding their rightful places on this fresh frontier.

We find out about this town of Bannack, Lucia's first home in the western wilderness, from an article done by that tireless writer of Montana lore, Martha Edgerton Plassman, who describes the Bannack of 1863:

There was almost no visiting among the women; four or five girls saw each other occasionally. No community life. Men found the saloon a common center and the dance halls and gambling halls provided others. Women stayed at home and generally found plenty to keep them occupied in the absence of conveniences. Marketing could have been regarded as amusement but marketing was not safe where pistol play was the chief amusement of some of the male inhabitants.

I made one visit to Thompson & Swift's general mercantile store when Plummer had an altercation there with another man; revolvers were drawn and I and others felt it would be safer outside. Shopping, it will be understood from this, partook of the nature of a foray into the enemy's country, and was not lightly to be considered. Among the earliest pioneers, men did most of the marketing and nearly all the gossiping, this amusement being theirs by force of necessity.

Mrs. Plassman further wrote that riding was the chief amusement of Bannack women, who wore long skirts and

rode side saddle. Berry picking was also considered divert-
ing, and reading was listed high among recreations. Books
and newspapers, which came from the East, were scarce
and the female population exchanged this reading matter
eagerly.

"There was no lack of excitement, however," continues
Mrs. Plassman. "Almost every week brought its news of a
stage robbery or the hold-up of individuals. Then, there
was the interchange of news between Bannack and Virginia
City; this and frequent local shootings kept social life in
a ferment. . . .

"There were no gardens in Bannack, as most of those
living there seemed to have forgotten that the earth had
other use than to hold gold."

Mrs. Plassman, however, does mention a beer hall of
this day which was especially gay on Saturday, payday for
the miners. She and her friends used to eagerly await Saturday evening when the beer hall's countrymen from Cornwall would loosen up their throats with the foaming beverage and then lustily sing selections from famous operas
and the world's best composers. These Cornwall miners
could not read a note of music but sang difficult arias from
memory. They often sang until dawn.

Mrs. Plassman agrees with other historians of this period when she writes: "Most of the women who brought
handsome dresses with them to the mountains, sold them
to the demimondes who were willing to pay fabulous prices
for them." The respectable women of Bannack and Virginia City, according to Mrs. Plassman, wore ample capes
and sunbonnets when they went to pick flowers or gather
berries. Prints, challis, and cashmere were also favored by
the pioneer housewives.

Emily Robertson Sorin Meredith, who graduated from

Hamline University, Red Wing, Minnesota, in 1859—she
and her sister constituting the graduating class—moved
with her husband, Frederick A. Meredith, to Bannack soon
after the gold strike there and lived in Bannack until late
in 1863.

Writing of Bannack in a letter dated April 30, 1863,
Mrs. Meredith observed:

I don't know how many deaths have occurred this winter,
but that there have not been twice as many is entirely owing
to the fact that drunken men do not shoot well. There are
times when it is really unsafe to go through the main street on
the other side of the creek, the bullets whizz around so, and
no one thinks of punishing a man for shooting another. What
do you think of a place where men will openly walk the street
with shotguns, waiting to shoot some one against whom they
have a grudge, and no one attempts to prevent it?

Mrs. Meredith said she made brooms of willow twigs.
Her kitchen was "well furnished" as she had a frying pan,
an iron kettle, a small cast-iron skillet, a coffee pot, and a
camp kettle. She paid $4.50 for a large iron kettle.

During her first year of teaching in that town terrorized
by desperadoes, when Lucia Darling heard a gun shot, she
never knew whether it was someone killing a pheasant,
a bear, or a human being! Cyrus Skinner and Buck Stinson,
two of Plummer's bullies, would get drunk and then start
shooting "just for the devil of it." One day, less than a
mile from the schoolhouse where Lucia was teaching a
class in reading, Skinner and Stinson, re-enforced by Haze
Lyons, another one of Plummer's terrors, attacked some
friendly Indians, killing several of them. Included among
the dead was a harmless, kindly Indian called "Old Snag,"
killed by Lyons, and another amicable red man, murdered
by Stinson. Both of these victims were scalped by the inhu-
man Cyrus Skinner. This was a trio that showed no mercy

to anyone, but who would later grovel at the gallows for a mercy surely not due them, and not granted by their Vigilante executioners.

While Lucia had been well educated and had led a sheltered life in her Ohio home, she reached out for adventure and fresh challenges. Her diary, which is now in the Montana Historical Library at Helena, reveals the romantic, poetic, and adventuresome nature of the young girl.

Of course lady diarists of 1863 paid much attention and devoted much space to discussion of the weather, but Lucia kept the weather reports at a minimum and seemed more concerned with the events going on around her, in the things that affected her personal comfort and safety, in the wonders of nature, and in the adventure of the rigorous crossing of the plains. Lucia's diary, in comparison to present-day autobiographies written on asbestos paper, seems quite prosaic and conventional, but because of her romantic nature that diary still carries the spirit of the West, written into it by a spirited, imaginative girl.

Lucia took her turn "on the watch," where she sat tense and awake the long night through, her loaded gun across her lap, watching for intruders, be they wild animals or humans. Of this duty she wrote in her diary: "While on guard last night, I kept my revolver close to me but wondered what I should have done if I had seen either a bear or an Indian. I mostly watched the willows waving in the moonlight."

June 16, 1863, more than two weeks after the journey's start, Lucia made this entry in her diary: "Our camp life has commenced and I am lying here on my back in a covered wagon with the lantern standing on the mess box at my head. Have pinned back the curtains so as to let the light in but it is so situated that I have to hold my book above my head to see."

Other typical entries from Lucia's diary:

"When we stopped at noon Aunt Mary [Mrs. Sidney Edgerton] and Hattie [Mrs. Wilbur F. Sanders] and I took a bath in the river which we found very swift and cold. . . .

"The fire in the little sheet-metal stove would not burn; the children were cross. The oxen were wild and ran from one side to the other—everything was in confusion to-day. . . .

"I hear there has been fighting on the Pawnee Reservation—the Pawnees and the Sioux against the U.S. Troops. Not very encouraging for us, just passing through an Indian country."

The next day, after recording the Indian battles, Lucia wrote this item in her diary: "We passed within miles of the place where the fighting took place. We put more guards on last evening. Some government wagons came on and camped with us."

Lucia was romantic, poetic, at times given to day-dreaming, and was always deeply responsive to the beauties of nature. This side of her is revealed in the following found in her diary:

The sky was a drinking cup that was overturned of old
And pours in the eyes of men its wines of airy gold.
We drink that wine all day 'til the last drop is drained up
Thus we are lighted off to bed by the jewels in the cup.

I might carry the simile still farther and imagine that the cup, filled with water, had been over-turned above us tonight for we had a terrible shower and our wagons would not entirely protect us from the driving rain. The lightning struck something not far from us and the wind blew fearfully.

Lucia looked forward eagerly to the evening songfests

around the big campfire, which brought the members of the wagon train together at the end of each day. At these nightly camp-sings, the weary but hopeful travelers sang their hearts out—of their fears and tiredness, their dreams and disappointments, their joy of survival for the day and their high hopes for tomorrow—usually to the accompaniment of one violin. The fiddler, according to Lucia's diary, must have had his proud moments, too, for often he was asked to play several solos. And the audience around that crackling campfire was an appreciative, non-critical one that found relaxation and restful comfort in the singing and the violin music.

That three-and-a-half-month trip across the plains did much to prepare Lucia for life on the western frontier. And later, more lessons on living and the law came to her through the actual hangings of the road agents almost next door to her home and schoolroom.

Lucia continued for years to take a leading part in educational matters, and always retained great interest in working for the advancement of education. She later married S. W. Park and made her home in Warren, Ohio. We're certain that there must have been meetings of her club or church group at which Lucia Darling Park reminisced, much to the joy of her fellow clubwomen, on "Crossing the Plains in 1863" or "When I Was the First School Teacher in Montana Territory."

Lucia Darling Park, indeed, helped to win the West, and from what we've heard and read, she was a fascinating personality, beneath whose serene, pretty countenance seethed a dauntless, bold spirit. Her merry, always dancing eyes were an index to a character that "dared and did." The very glow of her face reflected a *joie de vivre*.

Certainly Montana's first schoolteacher was no colorless,

prim old maid, frightened of garter snakes, let alone lions, bears, unfriendly Indians, and ruthless murdering road agents. No wonder Lucia became one of the beloved, colorful pioneers of early Montana; an exemplary woman who spread good everywhere she went but, nevertheless, enjoyed the whirl of the wild West.

5. Madame Eleanore Dumont:

She Had Her Own Code of Honor

In the rough, boisterous, burly mining camps of the sixties, which spawned such rich diggings as Alder Gulch, with its mushroom Virginia and Nevada Cities, and the Grasshopper, which inspired the founding of Bannack, first capital of Montana, the only hint of luxury, that which today is called "gracious living," was found in the saloons, hurdy-gurdy houses, and gambling halls.

The miner went from his wifeless, dismal hovel to the brightly lit barrooms, the gaudy hurdy-gurdy houses, the gambling dens. There he felt warmed, cheered by the brilliant interiors, the camaraderie of the card players and drinkers, the gay blitheness and friendliness of the hurdy-gurdy girls. He gambled, he drank, and sometimes he fought or shot his way out of a tight spot. He danced and often became involved, willingly, in a temporary romance. Next morning he returned to his hard labor with a throbbing head and an empty gold poke. But he felt assured there was more gold in the ground and he'd have it by that night—then he'd have more of the same in the houses of entertainment.

Beautiful chandeliers lit these public places, chandeliers hauled some 450 miles by Overland freight from Salt Lake City. Costly decanters were reflected in the big mirrors that covered the wall behind the bar. The backs of the bars, the frames of the huge mirrors, the bars themselves were all beautifully carved and polished. Men leered lasciviously or wistfully—whatever their assorted memories—at the paintings of voluptuous women scantily draped in filmy veils.

The saloons and hurdy-gurdy houses were the only places the miners could find music and pianos. Freighting a piano from Salt Lake City was an exceedingly expensive undertaking, and only the proprietors of saloons, gambling joints, and the dance halls had that kind of money or a place to put the instruments when they were delivered.

In the halls of amusement the miners also found the sharp exigencies of working and rough living softened, or at least dulled. Here the women in their frilly dresses and glistening jewelry smelled sweetly of perfumes and powders, and made the miners forget their harsh, coarse existence, or sent their minds scurrying back to the more comfortable surroundings of their former homes in the East or South. This was the only refining influence the miners knew, such as it was, even though wicked and evil at times.

Not only the miners but also the business and professional men of the mining camps dropped by for a dance, a drink, a card game, or to swap stories in these saloons, gambling places, and dance halls. A minister could often be seen standing in the doorway of some amusement house delivering a softly spoken sermon, but perhaps with his mind more on the gay scene and the shapely legs of the dancing girls than on his subdued tirade against sin. But the minister, 'tis said, never went beyond the threshold of these so-called "dens of iniquity," watching the hilarious picture unfold before his eyes—but always from a distance.

Writing in *The Gentle Tamers: Women of the Old Wild West,* Dee Brown observes: "It must be admitted that the scarlet representatives of the gentler sex played an important role in taming the West. As an old miner put it, 'Many's the miner who'd never wash his face or comb his hair if it weren't for thinkin' of the sportin' girls he might meet in the saloons.' "

"In one frontier camp," continues author Brown, "the saloon with its girls was the only real home the men knew."

One of the most distinguished, long-remembered and outstanding "scarlet homemakers" was Madame Eleanore Dumont, who operated a gambling house and saloon in the boom days in Virginia City, Montana, around 1863–1864.

Certain writers of western lore claim that there were only two kinds of women in the settling of the West— good women and bad women. The good women arrived on the frontier in the company of their fathers, brothers, or husbands. The bad ones came alone.

Madame Dumont, dressed elegantly and speaking with a delightful French accent, arrived alone in Nevada City, California, in 1854. Monsieur Dumont remained forever a shadowy figure, barely discernible as the dim figure in a faded photograph, a handsome man twirling a luxuriant mustache.

Within a few weeks after her arrival Madame Dumont rented quarters and opened a gambling hall where she featured a game called *vingt-et-un.* Her's was no ordinary gambling house and saloon, where profanity was tolerated, where miners came unwashed from work, where shoddy, broken-down furniture added to the general sordidness of the surroundings. No, Madame Dumont did things in the grand manner. She wore stylish, expensive clothes; her jewels were exotic. Her saloon-gambling hall was furnished in the best style of the day, with gleaming decanters piled in pyramid fashion behind the bar, their glistening beauty reflected in the huge bar mirror. Sparkling chandeliers gleamed overhead. There also were good tables and well-made chairs, and large, vivid-colored paintings, not quite suitable to the Louvre but above the average usually seen on the walls of establishments in frontier mining camps.

Madame Dumont prohibited profanity in her places. She also frowned upon gun-play and drunkenness. In keeping with the so-called "refined" atmosphere of her houses, she served free champagne to all patrons. While genial and friendly, nevertheless she usually held herself rather aloof from her customers. She made it a rule of the house never to gamble with anyone except those who wished to play for high stakes and who showed they had the gold dust ready at hand to back up their bets.

Of course, Madame had her moods. When times were good, she reflected fortune's smiling gayety and she herself was merry and generous. When she won a big pot she customarily and immediately gave part of it to charity. She was considered a "square shooter" and she helped many a miner who was down on his luck. It was generally known that when a miner lost his poke in Madame Dumont's gambling house, he was allowed to eat free in her place until he had made another stake.

Madame Dumont didn't run a brothel or play the role

of a courtesan herself in the good years. It was only during
the last waning years of her career, when she was broke and
discouraged and showing her age, that she sank to prostitution, and then she was on her own, never operating a house.
In fact, for many years Madame Dumont was admired in
the early mining camps as a good and honest business
woman, operating high-class establishments. Today she no
doubt would have made a name for herself in the business
world, using her talents in a legitimate manner. In any
era, Madame Dumont would be a personage.

She lived as graciously and elegantly as she could in a
rough and tumble era when men were men and women
saloon and gambling operators were the exception. She
seems to have managed triumphantly for years to do a man's
work in a man's world and yet keep her womanly ways.
She was only twenty-five when she owned her first saloon
and gambling hall in Nevada City, California. She was just
past fifty when she closed her own career, having won and
lost a dozen fortunes in as many gold camps throughout the
West.

In the hey-day of her activities, Madame Dumont was
a small woman, olive skinned, dark-haired, and immensely
attractive in a cool, aloof way, but with a certain promise
underneath it all if the stakes were high, her luck was
good, and the man appealed to her. Ahead of her day in
styles, she wore her curly, dark hair cut short, giving an
added softness to her piquant, flower-like face.

An interesting biographical note on her comes to us from
a former Californian, Daniel Harvey, who wrote in 1934:
"I knew her well when I was a soldier in the 13th U. S.
Infantry. I often played Faro and '21' with her. She was a
dainty, small French woman with short curly hair, parted
on one side. She looked like a boy. 'Twenty-one' was her

favorite game. She was married to Clubfoot Kelly, also a gambler."

Mr. Harvey, who was eighty-seven in 1934 and living in Buffalo, New York, when he gave the above account, knew Madame Dumont when she operated an establishment at a mining camp in Eureka, Nevada. His is the only mention uncovered as to her marriage to Clubfoot Kelly.

Madame Dumont was said to possess a rollicking sense of humor. Her quips were, it seems, more discreet than rowdy, but carried enough understandable humor to appeal to her clientele. She was known to be a pal of Samuel Clemens (Mark Twain), and he often dropped by her saloon-gambling house in Virginia City, Nevada, to toss bon mots across the gaming table to her—and then get them back, elaborately embellished.

Virginia City, Nevada, was the location of her second swanky gambling house, which she opened after spending one lucrative year in Nevada City, California, the site of her first business venture. Later she established several houses in the Comstock Lode country, and then moved on to the Territory of Idaho.

In the early sixties, no doubt late in 1862, Madame Dumont landed in Bannack, first capital of Montana, at that time a part of the Idaho Territory. There she conducted her gambling and saloon business in a low but roomy log cabin. Inside, however, the cabin was not crude and rustic; it had been transformed with Madame's usual flourish into a brightly lit, comfortable, inviting rendezvous.

Madame had not only a sharp eye for business but she liked new scenes, fresh adventures, so it wasn't long before she moved on to Virginia City, Montana, where she did business during the height of the Vigilante activities.

Will Henry in his book *Reckoning at Yankee Flats,*

writes of the Virginia City of 1863, the period of Madame Dumont's residence in that town:

All new camps are basic in their likeness, the one to the other. This one sat in a dry dimple of yellow dirt, surrounded by a welter of eroded hill-wrinkles, the whole enfolded in an ugly face of brown rock, scraggly pine and dusty brush. It had neither enough of water, grass, timber, law, love, religion, sobriety, hours of sunlight or good level ground. It was filthy, noisy, tough, exciting, sickeningly expensive.

You paid twenty-five cents for six dried prunes or a withered fresh apple; fifty cents for three pounds of flour or a loaf of moldy bread; seventy-five cents for a half-pound of coffee and a dollar for anything, from salt fish to strawberry conserve, which came in a tin can or a glass jar. Eggs were six dollars a dozen; chicken a day's pay for digging gravel; turkeys from Salt Lake City, fifty dollars and up.

There were practically no women except the working girls up from Bannack, and far too few of them, even at their ruinous ten-dollar an hour rates.

Of whiskey there was an endless variety, all from the same green barrel, and selling by the shot from fifty cents to five dollars, depending on how new you were in town, or how far above discovery lay your claim.

Add to this 4,000 frontier toughs from every state in the Union and sixteen foreign lands, including China and the Solomon Islands; shake well with equal parts of gold dust, greed and gunpowder; put along a five-mile stretch of a small Montana stream and stand by with a lighted match; there was Virginia City up in Alder Gulch the early summer of 1863.

Thus another landscape, "human-scape," of Virginia City is presented, although we differ with Mr. Henry concerning the number of women in Virginia City in 1863—all the authorities give the number "100 respectable women," and the population of the adventuresses fluctuated.

And this was the Virginia City in which Madame Dumont ran a gambling hall-saloon. "Survival" must have been her watchword, but she also made a valiant attempt to retain her much-guarded dignity, business astuteness, and fairly well-scrubbed reputation.

That she was a woman of action and frankness was witnessed to in her Virginia City, Montana, days. She always
used decent language, free of profanity, but the meaning
of her words, her orders, her edicts were never veiled. The
velvet glove could be very thin, the iron fist very effective
and apparent. She spoke "straight from the shoulder."
Surely that delightful French accent, which stayed with
her all her life, made her "call-downs" less cutting, less
resented.

She permitted no fights, no gun-play, no loud, blasphemous arguments in her establishments. In Virginia City,
Montana, also in Bannack, there were many fights between
saloon patrons, brought on by their hot arguments and un-
leashed emotions relative to the then raging Civil War.
Confederate sympathizers and deserters flocked to these
two towns and adjacent diggings, the Confederates no
doubt being in the majority among the riff-raff. This led
to hot words and hot firearms.

Although Madame Dumont was said to be a Union sym-
pathizer, she would have none of these discussions, which
inevitably ended in fist-fights and shootings in saloon-
gambling halls. First she ordered the men embroiled in
these unpleasant "disagreements"—how polite can you get?
—to stop their "wild talk." If they ignored her orders, she
had some of her strong-arm men, or "bouncers" as they'd
be called today, throw out the disturbers.

Her saloon-gambling house was open not from morning
to night but from morning to morning because for 24 hours
the streets of Virginia City swarmed with miners, gamblers,
hurdy-gurdy girls, road agents, courtesans, horses, merchants, and all sorts of vehicles. On the street corners, auctioneers cried their wares which they sold from open,
hastily constructed booths. The "barkers" selling women's
and children's shoes did a rousing, lucrative business on the

main street, which wound snake-like from one end of the hilly town to the other.

At night the big mirror behind Madame Dumont's long bar was bright, reflecting glistening bottles and handsome decanters filled to the brim. Outside, the town glittered from the lights flowing out from the dance halls, saloons, gambling houses, stores, and hurdy-gurdy houses. It sparkled as if a million gold dust pokes had been turned upside down on the lawless, wild, exciting town, the iridescent gold dust sifting brilliantly to the farthermost corners of this mushroom mining camp.

As Madame Dumont raked in a large pot of gold dust pokes with an effortless, graceful movement, her satin gown slithering, her jewels sparkling, many of Virginia City's notables walked through her doors. Bill Fairweather, one of the discoverers of the Alder Gulch strike, who threw away several fortunes, swaggered into Madame Dumont's saloon and later staggered out. He had paused to refresh himself after riding up and down the main street on his spirited horse, shooting his guns in the air, and throwing nuggets to the Virginia City children. Often he rode his horse into the other barrooms but *never* into Madame Dumont's saloon, as he feared that lady's sharp tongue.

Other patrons of Madame Dumont's saloon in Virginia City of 1863–1864 were, no doubt:

Sheriff Henry Plummer, the notorious, blood-thirsty, gold-hungry leader of the road agents, who was always dressed like a gentleman and, despite the evil glint in his glacial blue eyes, usually conducted himself like one.

John X. Beidler, who came not to drink or gamble but to pick up talk of the road agents, who became loose-mouthed and revealed secrets when drunk. Beidler, known usually as "X," was one of the organizers and leaders of the Montana Vigilantes. He, too, often ran down criminals by following up tips he overheard while listening to whis-key-inspired, saloon conversations. This fearless little man became known for his own special garb: a big white hat, a flopping coat (the duster type, much too large for him), and large high-topped boots.

The merchants, such as Paris F. Pfouts, who used Ma-dame Dumont's saloon merely as a clubroom where they visited with their friends and business associates, discussing business, improved modes of travel, the high cost of living, and how to best deal with the lawlessness that raged in this mountain mining camp. Pfouts himself was a leading mer-chant and a member of the Vigilante Executive Committee. Maybe Paris stopped too for a "quick one" in Madame Dumont's saloon, but only one, for he was known to be one of the substantial, non-dissipating men of the commu-nity, and notably talented at "flying on one wing."

Another first citizen who no doubt often paused cheerily to visit with Madame Dumont and talk business was Henry Gilbert, who in 1863 built the first brewery in Virginia City—and, as a matter of statistics, the first in Montana—just about the time Madame Dumont settled there. Henry, who later was to win first prize at the World's Fair in Chi-cago for his beer, listed Madame Dumont as one of his best customers—the lady always paid cash, 'tis said. (Henry's granddaughter, Sarah Trout, was the able and popular li-brarian and museum curator in the Virginia City Library and Museum.)

Another frequent visitor to Madame Dumont's establish-ment in Virginia City was Boone Helm, described by Pro-fessor Thomas J. Dimsdale as "a savage and defiant ma-rauder who died with profanity, blasphemy, ribaldry and treason on his lips." Helm was one of Plummer's most vicious and detestable road agents. He was also one of Madame Dumont's loudest and most articulate customers. Her patience and tolerance evidently had worn threadbare when this reckless and wild character came into her place one day and started some gunplay. Without raising her voice, and sans profanity, Madame Dumont gave Boone Helm a tongue-lashing that subdued and cowed him as no gun would have done. In telling Helm off, Madame Dumont also threw in some sound, free advice. She urged him to mend his ways, have respect for other people, be less quick on drawing his gun, and to cut down on his drinking and swearing. She denounced him as "a bully and a coward."

If Helm had heeded Madame Dumont's admonitions, he might have met a different kind of death. At least have been shot down rather than hanged. But his contrition, following her "dressing down" of him, was short-lived and he continued on his murderous way. (History records that Boone Helm in his lifetime killed some fifteen men, maybe more!) As he was hanged by the Vigilantes in Virginia City, just before swinging to eternity on the end of a rope, he screamed, "Kick away, old Jack. I'll be in hell with you in ten minutes. Every man for his principles—hurrah for Jeff Davis! Let her rip."

It was sometime in her plush days, and no doubt in the Badlands, that Madame Dumont took an interest in fifteen-year-old Martha Jane Canary, later to become the notorious Calamity Jane. For the elegant little Frenchwoman is credited with having taught the then teen-age Calamity Jane how to deal poker, and the fundamentals of "21" and Faro, which were two favorite games of this feminine cardsharp.

After Virginia City, Madame Dumont moved on to Helena, Montana, and later to Cheyenne, Wyoming. Then she took her equipment, her business acumen, and her likeable personality to the Black Hills country.

In middle-age, Madame Dumont's petite figure thickened and she became short, squat, buxom. The petal-softness of her skin was replaced by a leathery texture, and on her upper lip appeared a growth of dark hair. Immediately she was dubbed "Madame Mustache," a name which clung to her until her death.

As her beauty vanished and her luck ran out, Madame Dumont, who had never done more than drink moderately, sipping a glass of champagne or claret, took to heavy drinking. But as witness to her standing among the miners and to the awe in which they held her, even on her downward plunge, none dared call her "Madame Mustache" to her face. It was a matter of conjecture whether she even knew she had been labeled with this nickname.

During the greater portion of her operations in the West, Madame Dumont was discreet in choosing her companions. She steadfastly avoided underworld characters, shysters, road agents, drunks, and crooked gamblers. In Virginia City she did not encourage the Plummer gang to patronize her gambling house.

It was no doubt shortly after 1870 that Madame Dumont started going badly down-hill. She was well-known and well liked in Cheyenne, Wyoming, but it seems to have been just before her departure from there that she started drinking heavily. Later she dropped several degrees lower by offering her services to the construction gang workers along the route of the Union Pacific Railroad. But even in those days of alcoholism and promiscuity, Madame Dumont was careful about her personal appearance, although she could not afford the fine clothes of her affluent days.

She also remained kind and honest and still had a certain air about her that saved her from total degradation.

While she became promiscuous and alcoholic near the end of her life, she was never connected with any one man in a sensational manner, was never mixed up in any scandal or crime. Perhaps she did marry Clubfoot Kelly, the gambler, but no other mention of this marriage or even of a liaison with any other man is record.

Research reveals that writers differ on the denouement of the "Madame Dumont Drama." These two versions have been offered:

1. Madame Dumont is supposed to have committed suicide at Bodie, California, as she was found dead with an empty poison bottle in her hand. One writer, Duncan Aikman, in his book *Lady Wildcats of the West,* adheres to the suicide theory and contends that Madame Dumont killed herself because she was broke. Aikman also adds, "Perhaps someone called her 'Madame Mustache' to her face."

2. Madame Dumont went to the Panama Canal to operate a gambling business, as the West had become too tame for her, and in the Canal Zone she made a fortune. Then with her newly-made stake she returned to California, built herself a fine home, and spent her last years in comfortable retirement.

I think anyone who has delved into the life of this warmhearted woman would like passionately to believe the second version concerning the sunset years of Madame Dumont's life, but such a Pollyanna version must be sadly discarded when one reads the September 23, 1879, issue of the *Butte Miner* newspaper, which copied the following article from the *Bodie Free Press,* published in Bodie, California:

The inquest on the body of Eleanore Dumont (Madame Mustache) took place this p.m. at 3 o'clock, too late for publication in this issue. The drug used by the unfortunate woman, in taking her life, was morphine. Dr. Roe analyzed the contents of the bottle found by her side and it proved to be claret wine and the above narcotic.

Those who remembered the Madame will agree that she commanded a degree of respect very rarely accorded to one of her class, respect due to the traits of character which may be inferred from the following incident:

At the discovery of the Kootenai mines in British Columbia, Canada, the Madame joined the throng flocking to the scene of the new gold excitement and was among the first to arrive at the new camp, where the very flattering appearance of the diggings led her not only to invest all her spare cash but also run deeply into debt in erecting a large building to be used as a gambling saloon and dance hall.

But the camp failed to realize the expectations of its discoverers; the Kootenai mines fell into disfavor with the fickle prospectors, who were led south in droves by the fabulous reports from Carpenter's Bar, Montana, so that Madame soon found herself in the most dismal of all places, a half-deserted mining camp.

Nothing daunted, the courageous little woman packed up what little personal property she had left and took passage by mule team for fortune's new dwelling place in the great Westside camp of Montana. Here she prospered and made money fast. A year later the Elk Creek strike sent her to the mushroom town of Reynolds City and while there she met the contractors who had built her Kootenai saloon and to whom she was still indebted.

Having been contracted in a foreign country (British Columbia), the debt, of course, was beyond the reach of what little law there was at that time in Montana (there wasn't enough to hurt), while the contractors working there for days' wages would probably have laughed at the idea of presenting their bill. But, nevertheless, as soon as the Madame learned they were there, she voluntarily sought them out, ascertained the full amount of her indebtedness and paid it in bankable gold dust to the last dollar.

Truthful and honest, no matter what other faults she might have had, always smiling, never forgetting the politeness of her native France and her purse ever open to the appeal of sickness and suffering, Madame Mustache leaves friends in almost every class of western society to regret the sad closing of her life's drama.

This kind eulogy was printed on the front page of the newspaper in her last "hometown," Bodie, California, and reprinted on the front page of the *Butte Miner,* Butte, Montana. And many were the grizzled miners, the successful business men, the unfortunates, to whom she had extended a helping hand and open pocketbook, who dropped a tear at the passing of their friend.

Madame Dumont was a woman pursued, a woman running from something, ever driven on to new scenes, new ventures. Did the *something* from which she ran have its abode in her native France or was she running ceaselessly, frantically from *herself?*

Whatever it was from which she tried to escape, she kept right on running. This small, but dynamic, personage never retraced her steps, never went back. In the end, she was confronted with the disastrous—that is, disastrous for her—challenge of "the point of no beginning," and the only new adventure she faced was death.

So finally, exhausted, tired of running, and with her usual absence of whimpering, complaining, whining, she went out of this world alone, as she had lived—a solitary, striking figure on the western frontier, seeking the Unknown Frontier.

Thus the last card, the last bluff, was played by Madame Mustache, the once gorgeous gambling lady, Madame Eleanore Dumont.

She had fled, panic-stricken, from the seering follies of her past; the present made unbearable by drink and dope held only debts and loss of her one-time loveliness. The future looked foreboding, barren, stripped of all hope.

So she reached for the rich, red claret and the powdered morphine that temporarily relieved her physical and mental torture but eventually intensified the gnawing horror —and "cashed in her chips."

Who can put the label on Madame Dumont? Who can make the final estimate of whether she was a good woman or a bad woman, scarlet or white, or a rare blending of the two?

This recalls a brief but deeply thoughtful remark, laden with wisdom or perhaps even controversy, which I heard recently, and which seems all in the milieu of Madame Dumont: "A virtuous woman is not necessarily a good woman —and vice versa."

6. Mrs. Wilbur Sanders:

Hers Was a Respectability Fired by Courage

The forte of both fictional and factual authors has been to write robust reminiscences, suspenseful novels, and even harrowing tales of the loose women of the early mining camps, with a traditional and accepted tendency to steadfastly overlook the respectable woman. Such a woman was Mrs. Wilbur Fisk Sanders.

Mrs. Sanders and her small league of honorable women carried on as tranquilly as possible amid vice, crime, and rude, primitive living conditions; and always usefully, if sometimes a bit dully. They were the ones who crusaded for schools, and churches, improved morals, and worked for the permanent establishment of law and order. They were the ones who marched under the banner of "Blessed are the merciful for they shall obtain mercy," for these calm women, with their powerful influence over their menfolks, these homemakers, schoolteachers, wives, sisters, mothers, were also the very ones who cared for the sick and unfortunate, who helped establish the first hospitals.

These women were the unsung heroines who stood by their fiercely fearless husbands, the men who carved a living and a future out of this lusty frontier, risking their very lives to wrest a decent home and livelihood from the stubborn land and at the same time make war on the criminals spawned by greed for the ever-alluring and oft-character-destroying gold. These were hazardous years and these staunch women were no fools. They were well aware of the daily perils—everything from hostile Indians to murdering, robbing road agents—which their men faced.

Most assuredly these women who crossed the plains with their husbands, forsaking comforts and safety for the rigors and hazards of the West, had as Spartan hearts and stout wills as the male adventurers.

More loose women, more early-day western "molls," are immortalized, featured, and dramatized than the respectable women because:

1. There were more demimondes than homemakers, teachers, nuns, and other good women on the frontier.

2. The women of the brothels, saloons, and gambling and dance halls led more colorful, faster-paced lives than their cricket-on-the-hearth sisters.

3. The respectable women stayed quietly by their firesides—with the exception of rare souls like Libby Smith Collins—while the Annie Oakleys, the Calamity Janes, the Madame Dumonts, and the women labeled anything from "characters" to "wildcats of the West" wrote their own flaming autobiographies as they moved swiftly from one gold mining camp to another, as if pursuing some phantom fate or being pursued by something more real than shadowy phantoms. They became famous, or infamous, because they were expert marksmen, horsewomen,

and gamblers, were mixed up in robberies or murders, or boldly held a man's job in a man-dominated world.

4. It was unusual in those days for women to be in the public eye. Usually the females in the limelight were those under the swaying willow plumes or with men's hats jammed over their silky hair—to give the absolute farewell to femininity.

5. Loose women were more elusive. Dates as to age, crimes, or questionable means of livelihood were as written on the sands of time and swiftly and easily erased. It is difficult for the researcher to find actual material, bolstered and confirmed by existing records, on these frail ladies of the pioneer West. Thus the researcher-writer stretches his poetic license, always a flexible thing, to the limit and endows these hurdy-gurdy characters with virtues—and, we might add, an exuberant number of assorted vices—they did not possess, and dramatizes them in situations they never encountered, never experienced. The writer, however, can check-up more closely on a heroine who was a good woman of the West, who at least rated a dignified, accurate obituary when she died, who left a personal record—no matter how meagre—behind her.

Mrs. Sanders (Harriett Peck Fenn) possessed a respectability fired by a courage teamed with the greatest magnanimity, a Herculean cheerfulness, a quiet humor, and an indestructible resistance to any hysterical fears. Hers was a quiet, peaceful but far-reaching power behind a serene, soft exterior.

Her husband, Colonel Wilbur Fisk Sanders, a man to be remembered and respected, albeit feared—he was a grim foe of lawlessness on the frontier, the prosecutor of cold-blooded murderers, and an organizer and leader of the all-powerful Montana Vigilantes—must have caused his wife, Harriett, to feel daily the daggers of fear. Daily she was called upon to rout all such panic with a quiet determination, screwing her unmatchable courage to the sticking-place. How often this gallant woman must have lifted her eyes and her heart to the towering hills of Virginia City, to the unsightly scraggleness of Bannack's high rises, and repeated the Psalmist's comforting words: "I shall lift mine eyes unto the hills, whence cometh my strength."

To know this indomitable woman and to understand her panic-arousing problems, the pioneer hardships she cheerfully endured, and the crushing burden of worries she carried without complaints, one must first meet Colonel Wilbur Fisk Sanders, a Lincolnesque man with a forensic skill that Colonel Bob Ingersoll was later to describe as "the sharpest blade I ever crossed." Colonel Sanders likewise was a man of strong, decisive, and forcible actions.

As a young man he studied law in the Tallmadge, Ohio, office of his distinguished uncle, Sidney B. Edgerton, named Chief Justice of the Territory of Idaho, and later the first governor of Montana. Sanders and Harriett Peck Fenn were married on October 27, 1858, in Tallmadge. Two years and a couple of months later, early in 1861, young Sanders, who by then had been admitted to the bar and was practicing law, volunteered for service in the Union Army. He became a first lieutenant and adjutant to General Forsythe in the 64th Ohio Infantry. Just before the end of his second year in the Union Army, his health broke down and he was released from duty.

When Uncle Sidney received his appointment as Chief Justice of Idaho Territory, Colonel Sanders, his young wife, and two small sons, in company with Mr. and Mrs. Edgerton, their children, and other relatives, started the tedious three-and-a-half month trek from Tallmadge, Ohio, to Bannack, arriving in this wilderness settlement on September 17, 1863.

Hardly had Colonel Sanders established a home for his family than he was swept up in the Montana Vigilante movement, a movement born of the desperate necessity for survival against the outrages of the ruthless band of killers known as road agents, and captained by that arch double-crosser, Sheriff Henry Plummer.

On December 18, 1863, the road agent George Ives was captured by a posse of 12 men headed by Captain Jim Williams, a quiet little man with a reputation for being "all rawhide." Ives tried to make a break, almost succeeded, but was brought into Nevada City and a meeting of all the miners in the camp was called for the next day.

Two judges and a jury of 24 men were chosen, but of far greater importance was the selection of a prosecutor, Colonel Sanders, who was a comparative newcomer in camp and virtually unknown to the three thousand or more miners who gathered in the open air about the wagon whereon the judge and jury were seated. Sanders swiftly presented the evidence. Plummer was not present, but a score of his henchmen—all of whom wore the sailor-knotted scarf affected by the Sheriff—mingled among the crowd inciting dissatisfaction with the proceedings.

The Montana Vigilance Committee—later dubbed just the Vigilantes—had not yet been formally formed, but the men who were to be its leaders knew that this trial—an approximation of the orderly procedure in the courts "back home"—was to be a vital test. Therefore it was permitted to last a full three days, with four lawyers fighting for Ives and his companions, "Long John" Franck and George Fisher, and Colonel Sanders standing alone—and decidedly

unafraid—against Ives' legal—and, Ives thought, lethal—
foursome.

Describing Colonel Sanders in eulogistic manner, Dimsdale writes of the Colonel in these words: "The hero of
that hour of trial was avowedly W. F. Sanders. Not a desperado present but would have felt honored by becoming
his murderer, and yet, fearless as a lion, he stood there
confronting and defying the malice of his armed adver-
saries."

It was the night of the third day, the scene illuminated
by dozens of hand-warming bonfires, when at last Sanders,
knowing he faced assassination from at least a score of men
in the audience, forced the jury to find Ives guilty of murder and swiftly appealed to a viva voce confirmation from
the thousands of miners in the gulch and perched on the
hillsides.

Within an hour Ives was swinging at the end of a rope
and Sanders was informally made one of the three leaders
of the Montana Vigilantes, a leadership which was to
threaten the peace and security not only of himself but
also his wife for many months to come.

Mrs. Sanders had one unforgettable experience during
her early residence in Bannack, just a couple of brief
months after she arrived in the territorial capital. A dinner party was given by Sheriff Henry Plummer, and Colonel
and Mrs. Sanders were the first two guests invited, and were
designated as guests of honor.

What an odd social function this must have been, with
hospitality and gayety on the smooth surface and the black
undercurrent of evil deeds and deaths swirling like black
waters, below . . . a feast in the shadow of the gallows. This
Thanksgiving dinner of 1863 with Sheriff Plummer as host
is worth mentioning both as a sidelight on the brazen

crookedness of the sheriff, and also on the suave diplomacy
of Mrs. Sanders, who smiled through a dinner which she
must have known would be the last social affair hosted by
Plummer. Also, the quiet acquiescence with which she accompanied her husband, Colonel Sanders, to this dinner
party, when she knew it placed her husband's safety in even
greater jeopardy.

She and her husband discussed the wisdom of attending
or not attending the dinner and Colonel Sanders decided
it would be wise for his wife and him to accept the Sheriff's
invitation and conduct themselves as if everything was as
peaceful as an old-fashioned flower garden and merry as a
wedding bell. Colonel Sanders was convinced it was too
early for the Vigilantes to tip their hand, although this
law enforcement group already had proof that the Sheriff
was the leader of the road agents and knew he was doomed
to die.

Adding significance to the dinner was the fact that this
was the first official Thanksgiving Day, the one proclaimed
by President Lincoln in 1863, initiating a new holiday, a
new tradition; secondly, the turkey at the Plummer feast
was the first served in the wild, new region of Montana and
it cost $50, having been brought some 450 miles from the
"Mormon Settlement," Salt Lake City, to the gold mining
camp of Bannack.

The guests of honor were, in addition to Colonel and
Mrs. Sanders, Justice and Mrs. Edgerton. Other guests included the leading merchants and businessmen of Bannack,
and no doubt Miss Lucia Darling, Montana's first schoolteacher. This guest list was the most dazzling ever recorded,
up to that time, in the pioneer Idaho Territory.

But it was the host—the cheerily hospitable provider of
the $50 turkey—who made the occasion a diverting foot-
note to frontier history by his impudent bravado in invit-

ing Edgerton and Sanders to his table, for he, Henry Plummer, the young and debonair sheriff of the Montana gold camps, in less than seven weeks time would be hanged as the leader of the gang of highwaymen which had murdered at least 102 known victims to garner a loot of gold freshly panned in the fabulously rich Alder Gulch.

It was Plummer's superb affrontery which accounted for his Thanksgiving dinner, his audacity being spurred on by his deep, driving desire for two things that would seal his control of the Montana gold fields. Edgerton was the man who could grant his two heart's desires, for it was rumored that Chief Justice Edgerton would soon be named Governor of the Territory of Montana. Plummer wanted Edgerton to get him appointed as U. S. Marshal of the Montana Territory, and also to get him into the newly formed Masonic Lodge. The scheming sheriff figured that with these two desires granted, his position would then be secure, unassailable.

The dinner was given in the comfortable log cabin home of Plummer's brother-in-law and sister-in-law, Mr. and Mrs. J. A. Vail, with whom the sheriff now made his home. His wife, Electa, had left him more than two months previously, returning to her folks in Iowa, so Mrs. Vail acted as hostess.

It was quite a feast anywhere, anytime, but in the mining camp in the fastnesses of what most maps called "The Great American Desert," it was fabulous. Accompanying the $50 turkey were cakes and pies baked by Mrs. Vail with eggs costing a dollar each and butter at $5 a pound. Plummer poured French wines brought from Salt Lake City and San Francisco or St. Louis (via Fort Benton) and the meal was topped off with nuts at $10 a pound, raisins at $4 a pound, San Francisco coffee at $10 a pound, and cognac at $40 a bottle.

Plummer was most charming that night. He kept the

conversation going, saw that the gentlemen did not lack for Havana cigars and more of the French brandy, and expressed becoming regret that his bride of less than six months was not with them. Certainly no one watching and listening as he played host that evening could have believed his bloody history. But Colonel Sanders knew his evil past and he had no doubt told his wife. This happy pair, so close to one another, must have exchanged knowing glances over the cognac glasses, and then reviewed the dinner in the privacy of their bedroom, later that evening.

As the guests said their thanks and good-nights, Plummer could hear the music from the hurdy-gurdy dance halls, the shooting and brawling in the saloons, and he probably reflected that although some of the boys were having one hell of a good time that evening, he had had a better one, one that would place him in a top position where he would scoop up a fortune in stolen gold dust. The sheriff was feeling smug and self-satisfied, certain that he would be U. S. Marshal and a member of the Masonic Lodge in a brief time. He felt he had much to be thankful for on this first Thanksgiving Day.

About that same hour of the night, seven weeks later, Sanders heard Plummer's last pleas for mercy before he was taken to a scaffold and hanged by the neck until dead.

When the Sanders moved from Bannack to Virginia City, this latter town was in its heyday with more than 12,000 people crowded into the gulch, wedged between the towering mountains and one high hill to be known forever as "Boot Hill," where some of the hanged road agents still slumber . . . perhaps fitfully.

And here the Sanders resided while the murders and subsequent hangings of the road agents wrote a grim, stark, but necessary drama. Euchre and whist were the card games played by "ladies" in those days. Mrs. Sanders may not have known the rules for these popular games, nor even had had anyone with whom to enjoy card-playing, but she did know what the Vigilante sign "3-7-77" meant: It was the Vigilante warning to the road agents and meant a grave three feet wide, seven feet long, and 77 inches deep; it spelled death for these wild desperadoes.

Mrs. Sanders assuredly spent many fearful, restless evenings in her cabin at Bannack and later in the two-story frame house in Virginia City—one of two frame dwellings in that town—for she knew that her husband was out working for "law and order," that he almost daily was threatened with death by the desperadoes, that hostile guns were pointed at him during the trials of the road agents, that he had many sworn enemies among these criminals.

When she realized that he was one of the organizers and leaders of the Vigilantes she must have been forced to summon all her faith and courage to see her through those frightening nights alone, listening for her husband's footsteps on the gravel walk. It was the kind of waiting a woman never grows used to.

How she must have prayed when her husband was conducting the prosecution and trials of the road agents, when he ordered the Vigilantes to do their duty and pull the rope that sent these murderers on their final ride, sans guns, horses, or bravado. And if Mrs. Sanders asked that eternally feminine question, "What did you do today, dear?" she must have asked it fearfully, knowing the certain dangers that surrounded her husband. But she also must have been rewarded with exciting news of this rough-and-tumble mining camp, such as the trial and hanging of the handsome, but wicked George Ives, the first road agent prosecuted by Sanders; the devilish capers of Bill Fairweather, one of the discoverers of the lucrative gold strike at Alder Gulch, who threw away his money and died penniless; the positive proof given the Vigilantes that Plummer was the leader of the marauding, murderous road agents; an account of the peccadillos of one Captain J. A. Slade, who was "hanged as an example," and the subsequent fury of his anguished wife, Maria Virginia Slade.

As Margaret Edgerton Plassman, Montana's first newspaperwoman and apt chronicler of the early Montana scene, wrote:

> Life was more endurable for pioneer men, if constant excitement could make it so. Latest news from papers, rumors of new gold discoveries, were constantly afloat; reports of banditry and, as a last resort, politics, afforded the endless theme of discussion.
>
> The echo of this outside life reached the women, making their lot still harder by increasing their anxiety for the safety of their men folks. They could do nothing but nerve themselves to endure whatever fate would decree, which inspires a higher form of courage than is called for in battle.

And such a courage did Harriett Sanders display at all times. In Virginia City there was high tension, almost to the breaking point, during the Vigilante trials and the hangings of the condemned road agents. One day a man lay in wait to kill Sanders as he came out of his house. Later this gunman confessed to Sanders: "Colonel, you narrowly escaped death once upon a time. I was lying in wait to shoot you one morning as you left your house. But your little boy came out and called, 'Papa, come back and kiss me.' And you went. And I couldn't kill you after that."

Colonel Sanders was once warned that a certain group of killers, members of Plummer's gang, were armed heavily and hunting him down to murder him. His friends immediately armed themselves, offered to protect him, find the villains, and bring them to justice, but Sanders refused any organized help, and went out alone to meet his assassins. He covered them not with a gun but with dynamic, flaying words. Oh, perhaps the Colonel's hand was resting on his gun, for usually those desperadoes knew no language but that of a smoking gun, but he never drew it during his denouncement of his would-be assassins.

Virginia City, when the Sanders arrived there, had four hotels, three freight offices, two livery stables, one stage line, two doctors, three lawyers, six assay offices, a dozen hurdy-gurdy houses, a Chinese restaurant, a shoe shop, 20 open-front saloons, a half-dozen "advertised" brothels, several stores, the Wells-Fargo office, a bakery, a theatre, an apothecary shop . . . but no school, no church, no hospital.

The Sanders observed Sundays amid the noise and din that claimed the boisterous mining camp on the Sabbath. Every third cabin in 1863–1864, and for some years to come, was a saloon. Sunday was a gala day. The stores were wide open as well as booths on the street corners, manned by auctioneers who found Sunday the most lucrative day on which to hawk their wares—everything from kitchen utensils to ladies' and children's shoes.

The miners had the day off and thus the saloons, dance halls, and gambling houses did a big business. Horse races and impromptu prizefights also attracted large crowds on this, "the seventh day of rest."

Pistols flashed, bowie knives were flourished carelessly and dangerously, the crack of revolvers was the obbligato for the fiddlers' music. A $100 bet was considered small change at the gambling tables. The hurdy-gurdy girls charged a dollar a dance. Bad whiskey was 50 cents a shot; good whiskey, if obtainable, was double that.

The long main street was choked with men, wagons, saddle horses, pack trains, stagecoaches, covered wagons drawn by lumbering, slow oxen; painted women, respectable women; children taking in all the confusion and noise with bright, peering eyes and sharp ears; road agents, Vigilantes, murderers, robbers, gunmen.

And from afar came the reverent voices of Mrs. Sanders and her friends and their children singing hymns, keeping the Sabbath holy, following the Biblical commandments they'd learned in the East. The words from the Bible and prayer books, the songs from the hymnal, came in faint echoes, floating over the crude settlement to the far-away, majestic hills.

Early in 1864, A. M. Torbett, a Baptist minister, settled in Virginia City. Slightly later in the same year, the Reverend G. G. Smith came to town and opened a church. It was 1867 before Episcopalian Bishop Daniel S. Tuttle came to Virginia City, and met and greatly admired Mrs. Sanders, a Presbyterian, who, having broad religious views and an outstanding tolerance for all denominations, helped each of the above ministers establish their church.

While deeply religious, Mrs. Sanders was a woman who lived her religion in a kindly way. She was charitable. She was forever helping the sick, the needy. She never attacked, à la Carrie Nation, the gambling houses, the saloons, the hurdy-gurdy "palaces"; neither did she gossip and tear reputations to shreds. Rather she was constructive in her religion and also broad-minded. Since there was no Presbyterian church in Virginia City, Mrs. Sanders sang in the Episcopal choir and taught Sunday School for the Episcopalians. And even before the Episcopal faith was brought to Virginia City by Bishop Tuttle, Mrs. Sanders had taught Sunday School in her home, urging children and people of all denominations to attend.

Bishop Tuttle, who spent some thirteen years in Virginia City, eulogized Mrs. Sanders for her fine, broad Christian spirit, and spoke of her service in the Episcopal church as "invaluable."

In those early days of the Sanders' residence in Virginia City, flour sold for $150 in gold dust per 100 pounds. Eggs went as high as a dollar each while it was almost impossible to get fresh vegetables for the growing children. Even when available, such vegetables were prohibitive in price. In the winter of 1864–1865 the weather was so severe that freighting had to be suspended and there was a desperate shortage of flour. These were anxious days, too, for Harriett Sanders, since she had no more than drawn some peaceful sighs after the last Vigilante hangings than her husband took the lead in suppressing flour riots.

Harriett and Wilbur Sanders, like the young couples of today, must have often discussed the high cost of living, relative to groceries, clothes, and reading matter.

There was one bookstore in Virginia City at this period, operated by Daniel Webster Tilton, where papers, four-months old, sold for 50 cents each and paperback dime novels for $2.50 in gold dust. How Mrs. Sanders must have devoured those papers, with their news of her old home and the outside world, for her world in that narrow but noisy little gulch was hemmed in, cut off from the rest of the world by the lofty Rocky Mountains. In 1864 the *Montana Post*, the first full-fledged newspaper to be established in Montana, had a subscription price of $7.50 a year.

Shoes were very expensive, so costly in fact that many of the youngsters—and some grown-ups, too—wore moccasins. It's not too highly imaginative to think of Colonel and Mrs. Sanders patronizing the shoe auctioneer, who did his business from an open booth right out on the street. He made the bulk of his sales at night. There also was a

boot shop in Virginia City, a replica of which can be found
in the restored Virginia City of today. (This restoration is
a result of the tireless work of Senator Charles Bovey of
Great Falls, Montana. The restored Virginia City has often
been given the name of "The Williamsburg of the West.")

And the shoes! The ladies' shoes generally were fashioned
from plain leather, and most of them were high-topped
and buttoned. Sometimes the lower part was of patent
leather with tops of calfskin or fancy brocaded cloth. The
shoes were very pointed at the toes, much like the spike
toes in vogue today. Some of the dance hall girls and the
"frail ladies" brought fancy, pointy-toed, high-heeled patent leather slippers with them to Virginia City.

Mrs. Sanders and her friends favored plainer, darker
clothes than the demimondes, dresses simply trimmed at
the neck and cuffs with white lace. While the loose ladies
wore flashy trinkets, the respectable women's jewelry con-
sisted of small jeweled pins, narrow gold bracelets, cameos,
and tiny earrings for pierced ears; many of the pieces were
treasured heirlooms. Mrs. Sanders and her friends also wore
plain bonnets or small flower-trimmed hats; the gayer numbers, with cascading willow plumes or cabbage roses and
swooping veils, were the favorite headdress of the hurdy-
gurdy girls.

Most of the respectable women on arriving in Virginia
City, Bannack, or other gold camps immediately sold their
fashionable clothes, their "best dresses," to the female
habitues of the dance halls, gambling houses, or brothels.
How ironic it must have been for the women of Harriett
Sanders' type to see a gaudily attired hurdy-gurdy girl, or
even a loose lady, wearing the respectable women's clothes
which had been fashioned by some prim Eastern dress-
maker and worn only to church.

While Harriett Sanders longed for more books, more reading matter, and a church in which she and her family could worship, she also forlornly missed music which had been so much a part of her life. There were few pianos in Virginia City, and those were in saloons, dance halls, and brothels, because these establishments were the only ones who had the money to pay for a piano and the accompanying high freighting charges; also, they were the only ones who had a building large enough to accommodate the instruments when they arrived on the frontier.

On the western frontier, a piano was more than simply a piano. It was a symbol of the East, of home, of religion, of good manners, of almost-forgotten comforts, of memories of the past and dreams of the future. It was a rule of the early settlers that a man moved his wife first and then the piano. Often necessary articles of furniture were left behind so the piano could be taken to the new wilderness, it being recognized that a man's two most prized possessions were his wife and his piano.

All through Harriett Sanders' life ran the strong thread of a fine and understanding character. She played a dramatic role, although she played it quietly, in the brighter-hued life of her brave and brilliant husband. Hers was played to soft background music, the soothing strains of a Brahms Lullaby; his to loud, thundering Wagnerian strains.

While we've spoken at length of Mrs. Sanders' flexibility in adapting herself to the rough Western scene, of her Christian way of life, of her downright valor in never crying out when she feared for her husband's life, it is a deep look into this woman's heart to read her cheerful diary entries during her trying trip across the plains in a covered wagon.

Mrs. Sanders was twenty-nine when she made this tedious trek. On her mind always were the welfare of her two small children, Jimmie, four and Wilbur, two, and her husband, who had just been released from the Union Army because of his broken health—which was always a threat to her peace of mind. In her diary are daily references to Mr. Sanders' physical condition.

Mrs. Sanders' diary also expressed her admiration of the scenery, and she wrote of it in a most poetic manner. She also praised the food. A typical breakfast included fried venison, fried fish, cream gravy, pancakes, molasses, and coffee. She observed with seeming surprise that the children seemed in better health and behaved better than when at home. She told of taking horseback rides, enduring storms, fording rivers, bathing in the cold streams, washing clothes when the wagon train paused, and having an exciting time "watching those sharp-toothed, patient little animals, the beavers, build a dam."

On July 3, 1863, Mrs. Sanders penned the following in her diary: "This morning I wrung out my clothes and hung them on the wagon to dry. I'm surprised that they look so well. I starched the bonnets and put them over pillows to dry. We picked roses and sunflowers and morning glories and also collected some very pretty rocks. I have to take my turn guarding at night because of the Indians."

Mrs. Sanders described a squaw's funeral which the travelers in her wagon train attended, and she also told of making a delicious pot pie out of sage hens and grouse, and bathing, with several of the other women, in the icy cold Platte River. "Today I also baked 13 loaves of bread which was no small job" was another entry in her diary. "I made some gingerbread which came out very well when you realize that I had to make it without eggs. The boys keep fat and healthy, looking better than they did at home."

Mrs. Sanders always took the cheery view of life. She was a practicing optimist, the earliest of the endurable Pollyannas. Even when she wrote of storms, smoking sheet-metal camp stoves, the dangerous fording of swollen rivers, and the ice-cold baths, she did not whimper or complain. She just recorded these incidents as facts, as an accepted, natural part of the challenging journey.

In the immediate party with Mr. and Mrs. Sanders and their children were the Sidney Edgertons and their children, including Martha Edgerton, later to write under the name Martha Edgerton Plassman; John Creighton, a pioneer of Omaha, who later founded Creighton University; Amerette Geer, nurse for the Sanders' children (Miss Geer later married the wealthy Mr. Harrison, after whom the town of Harrison, Montana was named); Henry Tilden, nephew of Sanders, who first recognized Plummer as the masked leader of a gang of robbers who held him up; Wright P. Edgerton, son of Sidney, who many years later graduated from West Point and became a professor there; and Lucia Darling, who was to become Montana's first schoolteacher.

As Mrs. Sanders shared all through the years in her husband's worries, his heavy responsibilities, in the dangers that threatened him, in the hardships of the new West, she also with glowing pride enjoyed his triumphs and the honors he won in his public and professional life.

Colonel Sanders was the first senator from Montana. He was one of the leading Masons of that state; he organized the Montana Bar Association, serving as its first president; he was one of the original incorporators and the first corresponding secretary of the Society of Montana Pioneers;

he was the Department Commander of the Grand Army of the Republic; he was president of the Board of Trustees of the University of Montana. Outstanding in his profession, he was named Division Counsel for the Northern Pacific Railroad, and was also chosen a director of that railroad system.

Mrs. Sanders took a leading role in church, charitable, and civic activities, being recognized as a leader and highly respected woman in Bannack, Virginia City, and Helena, the three successive capitals of Montana. She and Mr. Sanders had five sons.

Mr. Sanders died in 1905, and Mrs. Sanders four years later. It is a challenging task to write extravagantly of this outstanding woman, who lived her life simply, modestly, yet heroically in the turbulent West. Her deeds, her very own character, seem to speak more loudly, more convincingly, than tributes. But in our research we found a tribute to Harriett Peck Fenn Sanders, printed in the *Butte Miner* of September 24, 1909, just following her death. It was a most laudatory editorial concerning the life and deeds of Mrs. Sanders, and it closed with this line: "Mrs. Sanders was one of the noblest women who ever made this commonwealth her home."

Who can say that Harriett Fenn Sanders led a dull life on this lusty, roaring frontier, deep in the heart of the rousing, stirring gold camps? And who would be illogical enough to contend that a respectable woman could not have a life of adventure in this wilderness, although its crime, vice, deprivations, and primitive living often left a gentle woman like Mrs. Sanders with a lonely, troubled heart.

Harriett Sanders was one of that huge army of homemakers who without fuss or fanfare helped win the West!

7. Maria Virginia Slade:

Some Called Her "The Lady Macbeth of the Old Frontier"

Montana was born amid war and confusion. Discoveries of rich gold strikes at Grasshopper Creek (1862) and Alder Gulch (1863) was news made known side-by-side with the reports of the battles of Shiloh and Gettysburg. Montana Territory was less than a year old when Lee and Grant met at Appomattox and arranged terms for surrender. During this turbulent time deserters, draft dodgers, scoundrels, persons not believing in war, those released from the service because of ill health, and those unfit for service flocked to the frontier, with Montana the most promising part of this entire gold-laden mining region. The snowy ramparts of the Rockies gave them cozy and safe refuge.

Captain Joseph A. Slade, a hard-working, daring freight-line official when sober and a wildly destructive demon when drunk, and his beauteous wife, Maria Virginia Slade, arrived in Virginia City in 1863, soon after the first gold strike at Alder Gulch. Virginia Slade took with gusto to the reckless, challenging life in this gold mining camp.

There has been much of speculation but little of actual record concerning the life of this striking, high-spirited woman prior to her marriage to Slade. The conjecture of her contemporaries—and it was not pharisaical, but casual, matter-of-fact, and therefore tenable by us—was that she had been a dance hall girl ("hurdy-gurdy" was the term in usage in those parts; "honky-tonk" was yet to come from the Barbary Coast). Other writers of western lore claim that Slade met Virginia when she ran a faro game (it was called "bucking the tiger" in those days) in a gambling house, and that when he got in a shooting scrape, she pulled her guns, ordered everyone out of the gambling establishment, and cared for the wounded Slade until he recovered. Take the story of your romantic choice!

Whatever her past, she was by unanimous account the most handsome woman in all the northern Rocky Mountain camps; she was tall, taller than the roly-poly Slade, "Junoesque," according to all descriptions, which means that she probably weighed a solid, busty 160 pounds or so, had "flashing black eyes" and deep-dark hair, and usually dressed her hair in ringlets, framing her arrogant face.

"Hurdy girl" or not, she filled the house (a stone house and not the customary sod-roofed log cabin) which Slade built for her eight miles from Virginia City in Meadow Valley with furniture which by today's collectors' standards was good, including a great walnut sideboard and a tall pier glass, framed with ornate, heavy gold. Undoubtedly, it cost Slade much unprofitable trouble to bring these from Salt Lake City, and when Virginia quit Alder Gulch no other freighter appears to have been willing to undertake their carriage, so she left them behind.

There is no doubt that she loved her little red-faced, schizophrenic husband. When he was sober she entertained at dinner parties, with candles and linen and silver tableware, and when he got in his worst scrapes she came to his rescue—except the last time, when she arrived too late.

Another favorite and shared pastime of Virginia and Jack Slade was horse racing, which was a popular Sunday sport in early Virginia City. As both appreciated a fine horse and both owned good horses (Virginia's a gorgeous black stallion from Kentucky named "Billy Boy" and Slade's "Old Copper-bottom," which got his master home, drunk or sober) and were excellent riders, they rarely missed a Sunday race. Wallace and Jackson streets were roped off for these races, where both the excitement and the bets ran high.

The exact place and date of the meeting between Virginia Slade, nee Virginia Dale, and Jack Slade is not known, but from tracing actual dates of events in Slade's tempestuous career, we do know that it was sometime in the early part of 1860 that she became known as "Mrs. Slade." At that time she rescued Jack from a band of his enemies who were holding him captive in a log hut, awaiting the arrival of the gang's chieftains to decide on the manner of Jack's death. Jack asked to see his wife, to tell her farewell.

Virginia, who was an expert markswoman, equally handy with revolvers and rifles, arrived on a fast horse. She was wearing a worried look and a voluminous skirt. Jack asked plaintively to "see his wife alone." The guards granted this request, and she flew to his arms. As he enfolded her caressingly, he felt the comforting bulge of two five-shooters in the pockets of her flowing gown. Jack still had his own two guns. Why the guards had been so careless is a matter of guesswork—maybe they liked the little guy! But anyway, he had them. He and Virginia rushed to the cabin door, each armed with two guns, surprised the guards, whom they kept at gun-point, jumped on Virginia's fine, fast-moving horse, and dashed away.

Also in 1860, the Slades befriended Widow Bartholomew, whose husband, Dr. Bartholomew, had been murdered by a couple of ruthless ruffians. Slade killed the two murderers, took Mrs. Bartholomew and her two small children into his home, sold her ranch for her, gave her the $523 he had found in the pockets of the murderers, and also procured a free stage coach ticket for herself and children to Omaha, her parents' hometown. Virginia Slade gave Mrs. Bartholomew many of her own clothes, and made over enough of her other garments to provide the two children with clothes for a year. Virginia, we know, was an expert seamstress as well as horsewoman, dancer, good shot, and excellent cook.

Slade was fired from his important job with the Overland Stage Company in 1861, and Virginia, historians say, had been with Slade for more than a year at that time. While excitement, high spirits, and an intense eagerness for fast living were all apparent characteristics of Virginia Slade, no one can discount or question her loyalty to her husband, for she stuck with him, not only in his affluent time with the Overland Stage Company, but also in that last turbulent, financially strained period, even to the day he swung limp and lifeless from the gallows.

Virginia Slade was a woman who took things in her stride, took them with disregard as to what the world—or even the Virginia City "good women"—thought of her. Her first allegiance was to Jack Slade—and she expected the same devoted loyalty from him. One story of the two relates how Jack, during their Virginia City residence, came home very drunk one night, and announced he was leaving her. She told him, "You took me for better or for worse and now you're not going to cast me off like an old shoe."

More seriously than playfully, she backed up her statement with two drawn, loaded revolvers which she held at Jack's head. He shrugged, patted her affectionately, and assured her: "Oh forget it. I was only joking."

She assured him firmly that she wasn't joking. Then, the episode was over. It was said to be one of the few times the couple quarreled. Usually Virginia Slade did not argue with Jack when he was drinking. She waited patiently for him in the Meadow Valley stone house, keeping his dinner warm for him, meeting him soothingly and smilingly when he arrived "falling-down" drunk. She fed him, put him to bed, cared for him tenderly. When he was sober, he took her to dinner in Virginia City, usually having his men friends as other guests, or they entertained at their home. Often when he was sober—or at least partially so—he escorted her to dances in Virginia City where she was the "belle of the ball," as she was considered the best dancer in all the Northwest Territory. He felt proud, too, as he stood by her side, whooping it up at the Sunday horse races.

One story is told of how Virginia Slade led a grand ball in Virginia City, her partner in this grand march being Charley Brown, one of the known and leading Virginia City Vigilantes. The story is that Charley persuaded another man to go to bed so he could "borrow" the sleeper's clothes and wear them to the ball.

At this soiree—for which a single ticket cost $25—the men were attired in a varied assortment of garments, either fine or shabby. Swallow-tails, riding jackets, winged collars, flannel shirts, buckskin suits, neckties, or bandanas tied around the neck in lieu of ties—all were in this motley display, and all were admired and accepted.

The women's dresses had very full skirts which swept the floor, and their figures were rigidly corseted, their waists small and cinched in. Red and brown striped material, flower-sprigged challis, and red and white checked goods, most in cotton materials, were favored by the women, only the so-called "respectable" women of the town being guests at the ball.

Virginia Slade's gown, no doubt made by hand by herself, was the outstanding one at this party of the year. It had a tight bodice, long flowing full skirt, and was of pale green silk, this alone making it stand apart from the cotton dresses of the other feminine guests. The pale green was striking with her dark splendour. She smelled sweetly, too, of lavender water, this and cinnamon cologne being the two favorite fragrances of that period.

The dancers whirled to such tunes as "Pop Goes the Weasel" and "Money Makes the Mare Go" and sang "Annie Laurie," "Villikens and His Dinah," and "Drink to Me Only with Thine Eyes." The dances of the day were the schottish, varsoviane, waltz, polka, Virginia reel, and quadrille. The married couples often arrived at these dances carrying a clothes basket between them in which nestled a couple of children—this being long years before the advent of baby sitters. Few single women attended the dances because there were few single women in Virginia City and environs who were rated as "respectable."

Virginia Slade was popular and respected in Virginia City, where, according to the mores of the early mining camps, judgments and acceptance of a person were based on that person's actions and deeds of *today;* the yesterdays lay dormant, undisturbed. Montana Supreme Court Jus-

Beidler, one of the leading Montana Vigilantes. Having dug the
[gr]aves for the three condemned road agents, he put up a sign read-
[in]g "THREE GRAVES FOR RENT," when they were saved by the
[sen]timental sob-sisters. (Historical Society of Montana, Helena)

Henry Plummer, who was hanged after the Vigilantes confirmed he
was a road agent in sheriff's uniform. (Historical Society of Montana,
Helena)

Sheriff-road agent Henry Plummer's scaffold. He had it built for a
horse thief, but swung from it himself on a cold, snowy January
night in 1864. (Historical Society of Montana, Helena)

A copy of the bill for $42.50, the amount paid to F. M. Thompson for making the coffin and burying Henry Plummer. (Historical Society of Montana, Helena)

Mrs. Nat Collins, who resided in Virginia City, Montana, during the Montana Vigilante reign of 1863-64. (Historical Society of Montana, Helena)

Mrs. Nat Collins mothering an injured cowboy. It was said that she could set a cowboy's broken leg, brand a steer, or deliver a baby with equal efficiency. (Historical Society of Montana, Helena)

Lucia Darling, Montana's first schoolteacher. (Historical Society of Montana, Helena)

Governor Edgerton's home in Bannack, where his niece, Miss Lucia Darling, first held her classes. (Historical Society of Montana, Helena)

Montana's first schoolhouse, located at Bannack, Montana. (Historical Society of Montana, Helena)

Wilbur F. Sanders, one of Montana's leading citizens of the Vigilante period. He held the first Vigilante court in Virginia City. (Historical Society of Montana, Helena)

Harriett Sanders, the wife of Wilbur F. Sanders, judge of the first Vigilante court in Montana. (Historical Society of Montana, Helena)

The home of Colonel and Mrs. Wilbur F. Sanders, built in 1864 and considered the finest home in Virginia City at that time. (Historical Society of Montana, Helena)

Joseph A. Slade's cabin on the Madison River, showing Slade at the extreme left, and his beautiful wife, Virginia, sitting in the window. (Historical Society of Montana, Helena)

This is the stone house built by "Cap'n" Slade on his Springdale ranch, about seven miles from Virginia City. It was here that his wife received word that her husband was about to be executed by the Vigilantes. (Historical Society of Montana, Helena)

This was the residence of Virginia Slade in Virginia City after her husband was executed. (Historical Society of Montana, Helena)

Hangman's building, Virginia City, Montana. From a beam in this building, the Vigilantes hanged five members of the Plummer gang. (Historical Society of Montana, Helena)

The original head boards from "Boot Hill," Virginia City, Montana.

Road agents' graves at Virginia City, Montana.

tice Llewellyn L. Calloway, who was born in Virginia City just ten brief years after the Vigilante reign, in writing a piece on "Cap" Slade, said of Virginia: "She had frequently attended the social gatherings, participating in the dances in Alder Gulch. She was admired and popular."

Like the other Vigilante women of 1863–1864, Virginia Slade spent much of her time in anxious, troubled waiting. She, like Mrs. Sanders, waited in anguish and misery for the return of her man. Mrs. Sanders, however, knew her husband was on missions, both dangerous and heroic, serving his fellow men, while Virginia Slade feared that what detained her husband was drinking and getting into some fresh trouble. Of course, she waited for him, too, when he was doing gallant service for the Overland Stage Company, but her hours in Virginia City were tense, troubled ones. The indomitable, trustworthy freighter, in those last months gave way so often to the drunken, obscene, swaggering Slade.

We can imagine Virginia Slade waiting for Jack. As the twilight closed in on Meadow Valley, she lit the candles. She knew that complete, velvety black darkness was not far-off and she hoped desperately that Jack was not far-off either, but galloping home on his faithful horse, "Old Copper-bottom." Jemmy, their thirteen-year-old adopted boy, brought in wood for the cook stove, then he sat quietly reading, asking his "mother" words now and then. Virginia peeled potatoes, put them on to boil; made a venison stew; cut the still warm bread she'd baked that day; filled a white jug with milk.

Outwardly calm, inwardly deeply upset, she went on waiting. Finally, she fed Jemmy and pushed the remainder of the food to the back of the stove to keep warm. She seated herself in a chair with some sewing, listening for the hoofbeats of "Old Copper-bottom." Many an anxious evening wore on for the dark beauty in her still, lonely stone house.

Like the other pioneer women of this wild, untamed West, Virginia Slade's story is only partially told unless the biography of "her man" is flashed on the scene, because women in this recently settled country rarely played a star part; theirs was usually a supporting role. Thus, to read the complete biography of dauntless, exotic Virginia Slade, who marched gaily but inevitably toward a dismal end, one must pursue first the saga of Jack Slade. He was either her husband or her man—no record has been found of their marriage. He is supposed to have met her in Aurora, Colorado, late in 1859, and a few months later to have married her in Denver, Colorado. While the accounts of their meeting and marriage are fuzzy, Virginia's loyalty remains clearly and boldly etched, not even worn by the passage of time.

Mark Twain met Slade prior to the little freighter's coming to Virginia City. In *Roughing It,* Twain writes that Slade was supposed to have killed 26 men. Twain and legend have stuck to that deadly number!

Slade was not hanged because he was a highwayman or a killer, but because he was a nuisance to the community. The greater intertwining irony was that Joseph A. Slade— "Cap" Slade—was more a victim of self-proclaimed and partially spurious notoriety than of the misdeeds he committed against the safety and property of the community, which, with some misgivings even at the moment, finally accepted him at his own self-estimate and strung him to a corral post.

Professor Thomas J. Dimsdale, in his book *The Vigilantes of Montana,* published in 1866, only two brief years after Slade's death on the scaffold, writes the following summation of Slade:

Such was Captain J. A. Slade, the idol of his followers, the terror of his enemies and all that were not within the charmed circle of his dependents. In him, generosity and destructiveness, brutal lawlessness and courteous kindness, firm friendship and volcanic outbreaks of fury, were so mingled that he seems like one born out of date. He should have lived in feudal times, and have been the comrade of the Front de Boeufs, DeLacys, and Bois Guilberts, of days almost forgotten. In modern times, he stands nearly alone.

But the critics of the Vigilantes' decision in the case of Slade, those people who come staunchly and emphatically to Slade's defense, ask repeatedly "Why? Why? Why? Why didn't the Vigilantes grant this man the punishment of banishment, seeing that he had never killed anyone in Montana? Why were Bill Fairweather and Slade's other drunken pals never even arrested or reprimanded, while Slade was killed? These defenders insist "Cap" Slade was killed, and at the beginning of Dimsdale's chapter on Slade is the anonymous couplet:

"Some write him hero, some a very knave;
Curses and tears are mingled at his grave."

Many Montanans had a genuine affection for the two-sided Slade, and there was a certain part of the populace who could be said to like Slade but not approve of him.

Supreme Court Justice Callaway wrote of Slade's execution, commenting:

Save for this [Slade's execution] the Vigilantes of Montana have been well nigh universally commended. For this act, they have been fiercely condemned and as vigorously commended.
The exigency seemed great. Was there to be regularity of human conduct in those mountains? Was law and order, so recently established in this vast region where there was no organized government, to cease and was all this which had been

gained to be lost? It must not be forgotten that the Vigilantes were patriots whose only purpose was to make their world a safe place for honest men.

Dimsdale summed it up: "The execution of the road agents of Plummer's gang was the result of the popular verdict and judgment against robbers and murderers. The death of Slade was the protest of society on the behalf of social order and the rights of man."

Slade is a fascinating case history for study by psychologists. Although in his lifetime, and during the lifetimes of men who had known of him, he was ranked as one of the most dangerous of all Western bad men, he seems certainly to have been a self-made desperado, a gun-toting bully who tried to live up to a legend which had been created around him and who doomed himself in fulfilling a fictional concept he himself had come, at least partially, to believe.

Most chroniclers fail to emphasize any of Slade's good deeds, such as befriending Mrs. Bartholomew, the widow of the murdered doctor; adopting Jemmy Slade, the half-breed boy whose mother was murdered; being a devoted, faithful husband to Virginia; his daring feats in freighting; his generosity in helping his friends. The historians seemed to have forgotten the humane reminder, "The faults of our brothers are written on the sands; their virtues in loving memories."

Slade was born, probably in 1823, possibly in 1824, near Carlisle in Clinton County, Illinois, of a very good family. (His father and brother both served in Congress.) The first legal record we have of him is his enlistment in the Illinois volunteer infantry—then called Foot Volunteers—which served in the Mexican War. After the storming of Chapultepec, he was listed as a sergeant, and is said to have fought with bravery and distinction.

Apparently he returned home for a period, then drifted restlessly, and with the inevitability of the restless in those days, to the western frontier. There is a persistent rumor that he "had trouble" from his killing a man with a rock, but it has never been verified.

The first definite record of his employment—he was a freighter, a jack-carpenter, possibly a farrier—is by the Overland Stage Company in 1858. Ben Holliday, who had been a partner in the short-lived but ever-romantic Pony Express, was the leading partner in this enterprise, which had a charter from the United States government to carry the mails from Atchison, Kansas, to Placerville, California. Holliday's prime selling point (and passionate purpose) was to cut the time-distance between the East and the West to the shortest that rugged drivers and frequent changes of horses could make physically possible. Holliday set the schedule at 20 days for the summer (roughly that period between the spring washouts and the first big winter snows) and 26 days for the winter.

It was a man-killing, horse-killing task. It demanded the sternest, the most driving of taskmasters. Slade had established a reputation along these lines, for when Holliday found he was having trouble on one of the most difficult divisions of the stage route—the 900-mile stretch between Julesberg, Colorado and Salt Lake City, Utah—he sent Slade to Julesberg as division manager.

It was here that Slade's reputation was born. Julesberg had been founded by, and was named for, a hulking French-Canadian, Rene Jules or Jules Rene or Jules Beni. Jules was a thoroughly bad number, even by the most flexible interpretation of the *laissez-faire* code of the West at that period. He stole from the company its best horses and mules and occasional consignments or parts of consignments. He stole from the travelers on the company's coaches, and from the emigrants and the freighters who paused at his post for supplies and repairs and rest.

Jules was notoriously proficient with fists and boots, but he preferred the safer method of using either his Colt or his shotgun to deal with those who objected, however mildly, to his robber-baron methods; by contemporary rumor, which is always subject to doubt, he had killed, or caused to be killed, several score of these, principally emigrants whose disappearance would not be questioned for months, if ever.

The cautious Holliday sent Jules a letter dismissing him from the Overland's service. Slade, either less cautious or less informed of the man's reputation and methods, arrived at the station on the heels of Holliday's letter and found the gigantic Canuck belligerently indisposed to relinquish his post.

It is probable that Slade did not realize Jules' nature when he arrived at Julesberg, for his first act was to go over to Jules' private corral and pick out, from descriptions he had been given and from the brands they bore, two company horses and a mule which Jules had reported stolen by Indians. He drove these over to the company corral and was on his way to the stage station when Jules opened fire with his revolver and emptied all five shots (they were five-shooters, not six-shooters, at that date) into the body of his unarmed successor. It's puzzling to this day to figure out why Slade had forgotten his firearms, customarily his constant companions.

Slade stumbled to his feet, tried to reach the safety of a shed, but Jules grabbed up his shotgun and let loose another blast. It was only then, with his weapons empty, that spectators had the courage to seize him while others carried Slade to a bunkhouse.

Slade had thirteen wounds, and it seemed a 100-to-one chance that he could live, but he was conscious when Jules, with two armed men standing guard to protect Slade from being strangled or beaten to death, called upon his victim.

"This will teach you," Jules said, "to stay away from here—and you can give that message to Holliday."

Slade, unable to move, almost dead from loss of blood, made a reply which may be apocryphal, but in its sequel was given general credence throughout the West. "Jules," he said, "I'll live to wear your ears on my watch-chain."

It is likely, with our knowledge of Jules' record, that Slade might never have left Julesberg alive had it not been for the fortuitous arrival, on the next west-bound stage, of several men who knew the French-Canadian's reputation. With a resolution the cowed station-hands had failed to show, they hauled the bully to a corral gate, threw a rope over the crosstimber, looped the noose around Jules' neck and hoisted him off the ground, not once but thrice.

Probably they did not intend to hang him, only to frighten him, and in this they succeeded, for Jules blubberingly—and gaspingly—begged for his life and was permitted to quit the station with one horse, a blanket roll, and his weapons on the understanding that he was to quit the region.

Slade somehow survived the jolting stage trip back to St. Louis, where surgeons patched him up and, after a long convalescence, was pronounced fit to go back to work.

But it was a nerve-shaken if not downright timorous Slade who returned to Julesberg, and now we see—in two attested incidents—the basic weakness of the man who was later to boast of himself as a "rip-snorting hell-raising terror." First, he went to Holliday and tried to get a transfer to another post, another job, even at less pay; but Holliday, a sedate businessman who shunned violence where it concerned himself, told him sternly, "If you don't go back there and settle it with Jules once and for all you'll never be able to hold your head up again. You'll be a laughing-stock, a butt for every half-drunk would-be bully west of the Mississippi."

Falteringly Slade went back to Julesberg. But Jules was still in the neighborhood, still vengeful, and Slade took his fears to the officers of the cavalry regiment stationed at Fort Laramie. They gave him the same advice as Holliday. From a letter written by one of the garrison, it is not difficult to make out that the cavalrymen considered Slade a bit too timid for the times and the job.

He was, in truth, antithetical in appearance from the concept of a bad man, a gun fighter, or even a man of resolution and daring. He was short, not more than five feet six or seven inches, and inclined to pudginess. His face was round and red, the red of the fair-haired who burn but never tan. His eyes were an almost baby blue (when they were not bloodshot from drinking; but that was mostly in his later days) and his whole aspect was ingenuous and inoffensive. He was, besides, a gregarious soul, an amusing raconteur by frontier standards, who loved to sit about a campfire and swap yarns and gossip.

This was, we may take it, the true Slade, the Slade who reappears from time to time through his subsequent career, the Slade revealed at the foot of the gallows.

But now we come, with bewildering abruptness, to his transformation into the character of Slade the Killer, the terror of the frontier; or, rather, the change in his reputation, or even his own creation of his reputation.

By the best accounts (and they vary widely, as we shall see) Slade offered $500 to anyone who would capture Jules and bring him into Julesberg. One story is that four cow-

boys caught the French-Canadian, but inadvertently injured him fatally in the process; that they brought him
into the Overland corral, roped the body to a post and
tried to persuade Slade that his enemy was "playing pos-
sum," and that Slade fired several shots into the already
lifeless body. The more persistent—and believable—account is that Jules was brought in alive, roped to a corral
post, and that Slade then emptied his pistol, his rifle, and
his shotgun into the helpless man, carefully refraining from
giving him the *coup de grace* until after he had slashed
his ears off and held them under his glazing eyes.

This is the version Mark Twain gives, and diaries and
letters identify Slade *en passant* as "the man who cut off
the Frenchman's ears." Whatever the circumstances by
which he got Jules' ears, it is incontestable that Slade did
possess them, carried them in his pocket and on occasion,
on drunken occasions, tossed them on a bar as warning to
those who refused his invitation for a drink for all hands.

There are those who go so far in their denegation of
Slade's reputation as a frontier bravo as to dismiss him as
a "one-notch killer"—that is to say, that he killed only one
man in his increasingly rambunctious and highly-publi-
cized career. But such a careful diarist as Granville Stuart,
one of the most illustrious of the founders of Montana,
recorded that in April of 1859, while he and his brother
were camped at Ham's Fork of the Green River near Old
Fort Bridger, Slade drunkenly killed, with little or no
provocation, one of the teamsters of a freight train he was
captaining through the mountains. Stuart also mentions
Slade as the "ruffian" of the ear-slicing episode.

It was because of this or some other specific incident, or
because of an accumulation of notoriety, that Holliday
eventually fired Slade from his job with the Overland

Stage Company. Some records claim that Slade put on a property-destroying, drunken brawl at Fort Halleck and the army demanded Holliday fire the boistering yet intrepid freighter.

He seems to have turned immediately to freighting on his own. This was considered a rugged occupation even at that time. The fast-rolling stagecoaches, heavily guarded, were seldom attacked by prowling bands of Indians, but the slow-moving wagon trains, drawn by eight plodding yokes of oxen, making at most ten miles a day through the tortuous mountain passes and across the swift-running fords, were comparatively soft victims for ambuscade or sudden raid, as well as richer in loot.

Slade—and this was a record which was at that time praiseworthy—never lost a man or a wagon. It was this record that caused the bankers, the traders, the merchants to seek condonation of his drunken outbreaks of ruffianism. But these wild bouts were becoming more frequent, more violent, and the man's ugly reputation grew and spread and without a doubt was magnified as it passed from station to station and camp to camp.

The increasing duality, the marked schizophrenia, of the fearless freighter now becomes more and more apparent, especially marking all his movements after his arrival in Virginia City early in 1863.

On the Jekyll side he was a hard-working freight contractor. There was not a man in all of what was then the Idaho Territory who did not know of Slade's almost incredible feat of salvaging the cargo abandoned by a Missouri River steamer at the foot of the Milk River. Slade transported the cargo through five roving tribes of hostile Indians all the way to Fort Benton, a distance of some 500 miles, fighting off two full-scale Indian attacks and delivering his load without the loss of man, ox, wagon, or bale.

To cap this historic journey, he brought his wagontrain down from Fort Benton along the rudimentary military road—little more than a pair of ruts—to Deer Lodge, thence across Deer Lodge Pass to the Beaverhead Valley, up Stinking Water and to Alder Gulch, completing a trip of some 900 almost trackless miles in three months, arriving on December 10, just before the first heavy snow, which would have closed all wagon traffic.

Thus we chalk up to Slade's credit his peerless quality as a freighter in those rough days and over those rough mountain paths, and also the love of his wife.

Now add up the red ink side of the ledger, the Hyde account.

Slade's all-out drunken sprees became more frequent and increasingly violent during that winter of 1863–1864. In a way it is understandable, for no freighting could be done while the mountain passes were choked with snow. He was flush with funds, and he was of the gregarious type which preferred the saloons and the whorehouses and the corrals to the placidity of the stone house in Meadow Valley.

Whether he was taken into the Vigilance Committee of Virginia City during one of his periods of sobriety and repentance is not certain, but it is doubtful if he was among the original signatories to the Vigilante compact and probably was admitted later. It may be, even, that he was expelled without his knowledge when he went on another of his sprees. If so, one cannot question the Vigilantes, for they were men of stern purpose and one member as irresponsible as Slade (when drunk) might have wrecked the enterprise at a crucial moment.

By mid-winter, when it was becoming apparent that the honest men of Alder Gulch would win their desperate gamble against not only Plummer and his gang but against all organized lawlessness in the Gulch, Slade had become an almost daily menace to peace and order, to the public safety, and above all to the purpose of the Vigilantes.

Then came that fateful, disgusting scene at the Virginia Theatre when Slade broke up Kate Harpe's performance.

A divertissement was being offered at the theare by Kate Harpe, who in the mining camps of the West had almost as great a reputation as the fabulous Lotta Crabtree. This special evening the solid burghers and burgesses of Virginia City and the surrounding camps were warmly applauding Kate Harpe. The madames and their girls, the hurdy-gurdy dancers, and straggling "frail" ladies of the mining camps sat in the curtained alcoves, the good women in the un-curtained portion of the theatre. Decorum was the keynote of the evening. The place fairly bristled with refinement; respectability reared its head most high—and haughtily. And the good people had paid $2.50 each for a ticket!

Into this sedate, decorous atmosphere came Slade, whis-key-crazed and staggering Slade, who stood up and shouted when Kate Harpe came on the stage to do a ballet number, wearing the traditional, multi-layered tarlatan tutu of a ballerina.

"Pull up your skirts," Slade bellowed. "Let's see your legs . . . We paid our money. . . . Let's see your legs. . . . Hell, there's a couple of dozen girls here probably got better. Pull 'em up. . . . Take off that skirt."

Alder Gulch's bourgeoise wives nudged their red-necked husbands, adjusted their pelisses, and stalked out. The unhappy stage manager rang down the curtain.

A warrant was served on Slade, then a second, then a third and a fourth. Ely and Lott and others among the burghers talked to him, and Slade, red-eyed and remorseful and boot-licking to a degree which disgusted these solid citizens, would come around next morning *craving forgiveness* and stumping up the money to pay for damaged, bullet-shattered lamps, broken windows, overturned bars, and doors broken down by the horses he and his companions had ridden into saloons and stores.

As far as can be discovered Slade and his drunken pals never extended this reparation to the women whose brothels they burned down. (What the hell! They'd paid the whores, hadn't they? Too, it was fun to see them jump out into snowbanks at five o'clock on a winter morning, and then go back into the cinders to sift for their money, their gold dust, and their bits of trinket jewelry.)

It is one of those minor ironies that the hooligan stunt which hanged Slade was the overturning of a milk-cart. To us, today, this may seem no worse an offense than a raid on a Good-Humor ice-cream vendor by a gang of grade-school boys. But in all Alder Gulch there were only three milk cows, and there were by this March of 1864 some 300 young children.

When Slade, with Fairweather and half a dozen other drunks, found the milkman's wagon unattended as he was on his pre-dawn rounds, they cut the horses from the shafts, turned the cart downhill, and gave it a shove. All that day's milk supply for Virginia City and Nevada City and the little camps in between went spilling and banging down the steep hillslope. Slade and Fairweather and the others thought it highly amusing, their drunken laughter mingling with the crash of milk cans.

Later that morning, when they had had a snatch of sleep and a few fortifying drinks, they still thought it funny, just a prank.

Even when Plummer's somewhat Falstaffian successor,

Acting Sheriff J. M. Fox, called on them, rather apologetically, with another warrant from Judge Alexander Davis, citing them to appear in People's Court, the jest continued. It was too good to let drop; they followed the apprehensive sheriff to Davis' office to have some more fun.

Slade tore up the warrant, saying he had paid "too many God-damned fines," and Fairweather handled the butt of his revolver and said, "I'm backing Slade's play." Slade threw the bits of the warrant in Davis's face and they all stumbled into the nearest saloon to celebrate another victory.

But fun had run out. John X. Beidler, the famous "X" in his last appearance as a member of the Vigilantes, walked up to Slade and told him to get back to his wife in the ranch on Meadow Valley. Coming from "X" this had a sobering effect. Slade sought out Davis and begged his pardon for his rudeness, then mounted his horse and was heading for home when his companions hailed him from a saloon.

"Are you going to let them run you out," they jeered. Reacting boldly to the taunt, Slade dismounted, went back to the bar, got drunker (if that was possible) and went in search of Davis once more.

By this time, although he did not know it, a dozen of the Vigilantes had gathered, discussed the question of what was to be done with the man, had differed because some of them liked and respected the sober Slade, and had agreed to summon the Vigilantes of Nevada City to consult with them.

Captain Jim Williams was at this time in Nevada City. The Nevada Vigilantes, who themselves had suffered by the hoodlum depredations of Slade and his booze-mates, passed their judgment and within an hour 600 armed miners were on their way up the gulch to Virginia City.

Meantime, Fairweather, possibly because of a warning from those who still thought of him as the man who had made the strike, disappeared with a prudence uncommon to him, but Slade had lurched in and out of stores until he had found Davis.

Davis was talking to Paris Pfouts, President of the Vigilantes, and Slade did not know it but Davis was trying to persuade Pfouts to ask the other leading Vigilantes to rescind the judgment against Slade.

Slade pulled out the derringer with which he had threatened so many men, grabbed Davis by the arm, and demanded, "Is it true? Are they coming up from Nevada? If it is, if anybody tries to get me, they'll have to shoot you before they get to me."

Then the basic Slade reappears: He begs Davis' pardon, he begs Pfouts' pardon, he pleads that he didn't know what he did when he was drunk, that he had always made restitution and apologies, that everyone knew he was an honest man, a freighter without equal, a loving husband.

He is still at his protestations, his apologies, when Williams and the vanguard of the men from Nevada walk in, and the ordinarily mild Williams, now once again icy-eyed, tells him that the whole community, the length of the gulch, has decided that he has had not one but several too many chances.

At once the great myth of Slade the killer, the frontier bravo, "the most feared man west of Julesberg," dissolves. Slade crawls, literally. On his knees he goes from one to another, reminding them of old comradeship, ever and again speaking of his wife, "My poor wife."

Pfouts and John Lott, who had taken it upon themselves to warn him again and again, have washed their hands of him. Colonel Wilbur F. Sanders, who has prosecuted 19 of the Plummer gang, gives a silent stern nod. Davis, who had had his warrant flung in his face, who had had Slade's derringer in his ribs ten minutes earlier, Davis alone pleads that the sentence be mitigated to banishment. Williams shakes his head, and the men with shotguns and rifles haul Slade to his feet and lead him to the corral behind the store.

There, under the cross-bar of the corral gate, where usually beef were tied to cool before butchering, pot-bellied little Slade reverts to type, repudiates the reputation he had cherished, nourished, flaunted, and once more gets on his knees in the cow dung and mud to plead for his life. They may cut off his hands, cut off his feet, cut out his tongue, gouge out his eyes, put him on a brokendown mule and send him without food or weapons across the mountains . . . but, please, please, mercy of God, don't hang him! . . . "My wife . . . my dear wife. . . ."

Sanders almost sickened. The others had stronger stomachs.

Slade was playing one desperate card against time and the rope: "My dear wife."

Someone (it never was known who—perhaps Jim Kiskadden) had sent a messenger at breakneck speed to Meadow Valley, and Virginia, the strong-bodied, dark-browed Virginia, who could ride and shoot as few men could, caught up her Kentucky blood horse and rode for the gulch with her hair streaming.

But the men who had determined upon Slade's end knew Virginia too well, knew the appeal she would make, the effect she might have on these rough but essentially susceptible miners, and somehow word got to them that the message of her husband's plight had been sent to her.

They did not delay, and because they did not the history of the Vigilantes ended, as Slade's life ended, just as the furious woman, her hair loose, her horse half-dead, topped the last ridge that led down into Virginia City.

The crowd melted before her fury and her grief. Only a few old friends stood beside the body in the Virginia Hotel. These friends, including J. M. Kiskadden, whom Virginia later married, had cut Slade down, cut off the ropes at knee and ankle, covered him decently. Slade's body was still warm when Virginia threw herself from the saddle and flung herself upon the body of the roly-poly, periodic drunkard.

Virginia, grief-stricken and bitter as she gazed on her dead husband, shrieked at those around the death-bed: "Why, oh, why didn't one of you shoot him, not let him endure the shame of being hanged? If I had been here, I would have done it. No dog's death should have come to such a man. He did not deserve to die on the scaffold."

She was so bitter against Montana, Virginia City, and especially the Vigilantes, contending that her husband was a charter member of the Vigilantes, that she refused to allow him to be buried in Montana soil. She had a zinc coffin especially built and ironically had the body preserved in alcohol, and then had the coffin temporarily buried across the road from the stone house in Meadow Valley, placing the grave where she could gaze on it from her largest window. This was in February, and it was not until summer that she was able to take the body to Salt Lake City for burial. He was buried on July 20, 1864, in the old Salt Lake Cemetery.

One can easily picture that dreary winter, the depression not even lifting with the coming of soft spring days, when Virginia Slade sat in the stone house peopled with the ghosts of the man she loved—Slade attentive and loving; Slade admiring her pale green silk ball gown, himself dressed in his best to take her to the ball in Virginia City; Slade, the generous and genial dinner host; Slade, the affectionate admiring husband; Slade, buying her gifts with the happiness of a child acquiring a new toy; Slade taking her to the Sunday horse races.

During this bleak time she had as her only companion the handsome half-breed Indian boy Jemmy, whom she and Slade had unofficially adopted. Snowballing rumor said that Slade had killed the boy's white father in one of his sprees and then adopted the boy in contrition, but Virginia Slade fiercely denied this story.

Slade had many friends, despite his carousings, and some of them were the most prominent men, such as Paris S. Pfouts, the first mayor of Virginia City, who greatly respected and admired Virginia and had a deep affection for the odd, mixed-up little Jekyll-Hyde character, "Cap" Slade. Perhaps the most frequent of her callers was Kiskadden, who was both a gambler and mining man, and a friend of Slade's of long standing. He immediately liked Virginia Slade and became her staunch friend. After Slade's death, Jim Kiskadden was her suitor, later husband.

First mention we find of Kiskadden in the lives of the Slades was when "Cap" and Virginia arrived in Virginia City, and Kiskadden and Slade renewed their old friendship. The Slades lived at the Virginia City Hotel until their first home, a frame-house, was completed at Ravenswood, and they ate at the hotel and the Chinese restaurant. Kiskadden often made it a dinner trio, and after the Slades were settled at Ravenswood, where they lived only briefly, he often rode his horse out in the valley to be a dinner guest of his old friend and his striking, brunette wife.

It is an established fact that Kiskadden often hauled the whiskey-soaked, trouble-making Slade out of bars, brothels, and dance halls, and took him home. He liked Slade and his lovely wife but it was all on a friendship basis, as far as Virginia was concerned, until after Slade's hanging.

The story of Slade's last Christmas, in 1863, was one of disappointment and worry for his wife, according to certain chroniclers, and this Yuletide account sounds very plausible. Virginia planned a festive Christmas party for her husband and young Jemmy, to which Jim Kiskadden and several of Slade's friends were invited. Her best linen was immaculate; the dinnerware shone. She had trimmed a pine tree with strings of popcorn and festooned with chains of colored paper, and she hung balls of cotton, sprinkled with irridescent powder, on the boughs. They were to undo the presents that the guests had brought for young Jemmy, drink friendly toasts, and eat the fine dinner Virginia had prepared.

The guests arrived in a gay holiday mood but their spirits waned as the day wore on, twilight settled over the valley, and still no Slade. Finally the guests, Virginia, and Jemmy ate a quiet dinner, having tired of trying to be merry while looking at the vacant chair, and imagining the grim, drunken, dark happenings which detained Slade. The guests left before the celebrating Slade arrived home.

It was also Kiskadden who tried so insistently but unsuccessfully to get Slade to go home when he was writing his own hanging ticket by insulting officials, destroying property, and resisting the law. It was Kiskadden, too, who pleaded for Jack's life at the foot of the gallows. It was Kiskadden, the faithful family friend, who heard that Virginia was riding to town—it was even said that Kiskadden sent for her to come to her husband's rescue—and who hurriedly gathered men to help him move Jack's body to the best room in the Virginia Hotel. And it was

Kiskadden who escorted the grieving widow to the now silent Slade stone house in Meadow Valley.

Kiskadden, it is logical to believe, called often on the saddened widow as she sat in that tranquil stone house, which no longer echoed to the rollicking laughter of the little paunchy man whom she had loved so deeply and loyally. How cold the finality of death, Virginia must have mused, as the pine trees sighed out their funeral dirge over Jack's grave.

After Virginia returned to Virginia City from taking her husband's body to Salt Lake City for burial, she never returned to the stone house. She sold the ranch and Slade's freighting outfit for $7,000. She probated his will, this being the first will probated in the Montana Territory. Then she settled in a one-and-a-half-story frame house in Virginia City (a house that was later to be the Methodist parsonage) and lived there quietly, if somewhat bitterly, until the following March, a little over a year after her husband's execution, when she married Jim Kiskadden.

Virginia and Jim Kiskadden were married on March 22, 1865, at Virginia's home by H. S. Hosmer, Chief Justice of the Supreme Court of Montana Territory. The wedding was reported in the *Montana Post* of that date. It told of a wedding reception at the bride's home and of two golden "V's" imbedded in the two beautiful wedding cakes at the reception. And the paper, which played up the account of the wedding on its front page, extended well wishes to the couple, the report of their marriage containing this message: "May you and your amiable bride enjoy many long years of happiness and content. May the pathway in life's journey be smooth and the end far-off."

The newlyweds left immediately for Salt Lake City where they made their home. But the end was not "far-off."

While they had had a most pleasant friendship, devoid of all quarrels, their married life was, after a few months, sprinkled with heated arguments and violent quarrels.

It's said that Kiskadden became scared of Virginia and her violence. Just before they parted, he told his friends: "Virginia is a very desperate woman."

High spirited and daring she had been, but no doubt this extreme violence, this desperation, was born of the bitterness she suffered after Slade's execution, an execution which she considered unfair, uncalled for, and even vicious on the part of the Vigilantes, many of whom were supposed to be Slade's friends. Also, the fact that Slade was executed and none of his destructive cohorts were even arrested, outraged Virginia's code of fairness. So the Kiskaddens parted after a year of marriage.

Kiskadden got his divorce March 12, 1868. Later he married Annie Adams, a Salt Lake City actress, and their daughter was the celebrated Maude Adams, of "Peter Pan" fame.

Whether Virginia Slade died in Omaha or Chicago is not known, but chroniclers do agree that Virginia Slade Kiskadden, once the most beautiful woman—the best dancer, the best horsewoman, the best shot in all the Northwest Territory—was running a brothel in one of those two towns when she died. Thus it seems that with the death of Slade, the valiant spirit within this dauntless woman also died, as did her dreams.

Some women lived high wide and handsome, others led as calm, tranquil, and conventional lives as possible in the western wilderness. Virginia Slade while in Virginia City no doubt curbed her daring tendencies and attempted to live a decent life, be a loyal wife, and a good mother to the adopted Jemmy. After her husband's execution, she fostered her deep venom and hatred, which consumed her best qualities, leading her on to her own doom and destruction; Virginia Slade could not live and dance and dream without her "Cap" Slade. Thus, when he swung from the gallows, her destiny, her tragic defeat, was written. So it would seem that the demise of Joseph A. Slade was virtually a double hanging . . . and was it necessary?

When the deep blackness of night settles over Meadow Valley, sometimes softened to a dull gray by the gathering of the mists, or punctured by the rays of a silver-white moon, it is said that Virginia Slade swoops through the dale, riding her black stallion covered with foam, her black silk dress billowing in the wind, her hair floating in black streams behind her, her face a dead white, her wild screams tearing apart the eerie stillness of the valley. Her cries pleading for the Vigilantes to spare her husband are said, in their chill dreadfulness, to echo to the very top of the Tobacco Root Mountains. Those who recite this saga of Virginia Slade's weird night-ride always shudder and declare "They say it's a horrible sight . . . and those terrible shrieks can be heard for miles around."

Legend has it that two sheepherders stopped one night at the Slade house in Meadow Valley, and they were found dead in the morning. Travelers and curiosity seekers since then have not tarried there after nightfall.

The partial ruins of the stone dwelling, however, still stand. Half of the building has been destroyed by persons seeking gold, believing tales that the Slades buried gold dust under the house. The other half of the house has given way to the deterioration of time.

But, even the most skeptical residents of old Alder Gulch, especially of Virginia City, shake their heads won-

deringly whenever they hear the legend of the raven-haired Virginia, galloping in darkness on her black horse, crying for the life of the man she loved, and they recall that in some parts of the western wilderness she was known as "The Lady Macbeth of the Old Frontier."

To those who believe in ghosts, this chilling legend is plausible; to those who scoff at spooks—well, they also keep away from the Slade house in the darkness of the night!

8. Mrs. Thomas J. (Annette) Dimsdale Foster:

A Lady Who Was Almost By-Passed by Western History

In the early days of the West, legends flew with the frequency of bullets. And some of them were just as wild.

The legend of Professor Thomas J. Dimsdale is a case in point. In most of the official histories of Montana, Dimsdale is pictured as a pallid, consumptive bachelor who viewed and recorded the blood-and-thunder days of the Montana Vigilantes with journalistic precision and the detachment forced by ill health.

Facts, though sparse and unsatisfying yet authentic, have come to life which turn the anemic bachelor into a rather luxurious frontiersman.

Scant but exciting records have revealed that this First Gentleman of Montana Territory during the Vigilante reign was a married man! Biographies to the contrary!

Most biographies will tell you that Thomas J. Dimsdale was an Oxford man who came from England to Canada and then down to the Idaho Territory, settling in Virginia City. Some biographers contend that he left England because of poor health and was urged to live in the mountains. Others say his debtors were breathing hot down his neck. Other writers contend it was a combination of the two—ill health and unpaid bills.

Anyway, these Dimsdale chroniclers all agree that he arrived in Virginia City by way of Canada in 1863. In *An Introduction to the Vigilantes of Montana*—a fourth printing done in 1936 by the University of Oklahoma Press— E. De Golyer, one of the country's best-known collectors of western Americana, and an authority on western non-fiction, writes this of Professor Dimsdale:

The author, Thomas J. Dimsdale, was an educated Englishman and one-time Oxonian who arrived in Virginia City via Canada during the summer of 1863. He suffered from consumption and had come to the mountains seeking health. During the winter of 1863-64 he taught a private school, tuition $2.00 a week for each pupil, and also conducted a singing school. A man of culture and refinement, he drew to himself all that was best of the society of that time in Virginia City. He is described by Granville Stuart as "a gentle, kind-hearted Christian man."

Montana was organized as a Territory on May 26, 1864, with Bannack as temporary capital. Governor Edgerton appointed Dimsdale the first Superintendent of Public Instruction. He also became the first editor of the *Montana Post*, the first newspaper of consequence to be published in the territory. Its press and equipment were brought from St. Louis to Fort Benton by River, thence by wagon to Virginia City.

Dimsdale wrote *Vigilantes of Montana* as a series of articles, the first of which were published in the *Post*, August 26, 1865.

The articles were collected and republished in a paper bound book in 1866, the first book to be published in Montana. Copies of this book are superlatively rare. Dimsdale died September 22, 1866, at the age of thirty-five, mourned by all who knew him.

Note there is no mention of a marriage, a wife, or personal life in this estimate of Dimsdale.

During our years of research we never found Professor Dimsdale's wife Annette (or, as she was called in Virginia City, "Nettie") mentioned. In his chapter on "Dillingham's Murderers" in *The Vigilantes of Montana,* Dimsdale wrote: "A woman is a queen in her own home." Perhaps Mr. Dimsdale did not believe in the queen wandering far from her throne. Yet in the obituary on Nettie published in the August 29, 1874, issue of the *New North-West,* of Deer Lodge, Montana, one reads: "Living at Virginia City during the reign of the Vigilantes, she [Mrs. Dimsdale] was an eye witness to many of the wild scenes daily occurring, and had, perhaps, more experience in the hardships and excitements of pioneer life than any other woman in Montana. Brave and generous, she had many warm and true friends, who will be pained to hear of her death."

So Nettie Dimsdale must have been active outside her own home. She must have taken part in the town's activities, must have had many friends and acquaintances there.

The worn-out phrase "There's always a good woman behind every successful man"—never saying whether she's patting him with a gentle hand or prodding him with a kitchen knife—could come into its own here, because Mrs. Dimsdale might have been Tom's silent partner.

She could have gathered items for his newspaper, the *Montana Post,* the first full-fledged newspaper in Montana with Dimsdale as the first newspaper editor in that area. She could have covered the Halloween Ball, a theatre party, a dinner honoring Governor Edgerton. Perhaps she helped bring some of the village children into the world, and thus wrote a birth column. She, no doubt, laid out some poor soul, and then composed the obituary for the *Montana Post*. She might have even proofread his first book.

Nettie surely could have been of great help to this "Man of Many Firsts," her assistance going far beyond mending his socks and cooking his favorite meal, roast beef and Yorkshire pudding.

Dimsdale's opinions on women and their place—or rather their lack of place—in the outside world were well defined in *Vigilantes of Montana*. The passages in which he wrote so chidingly of the role the women folks played in getting Dillingham's murderers freed were quoted earlier in this book. That's where he brings out the women-should-stay-at-home cliché.

In recording the murder of old Chief Snag at Bannack by a bunch of drunks gone berserk, Dimsdale wrote:

While the firing was going on, two ladies were preparing for a grand ball supper in the house adjoining the scene of the murder of Snag. The husband of one of them being absent, cutting house logs among the timber, his wife, alarmed for his safety, ran out with her arms and fingers extended with soft paste. She jumped the ditch at a bound, her hair streaming in the wind, and shouted aloud "Where's Mr. ——? Will nobody fetch me my husband?" We are happy to relate that the object of her tender solicitude turned up uninjured, and if he was not grateful for this display of affection, we submit to the ladies, without any fear of contradiction, that he must be a monster.

Could Tom have been thinking of his Nettie and her continued tender solicitude for him when he wrote the above? Could he have been dreaming of his Nettie, and, grown softly sentimental, become convinced that she, too, would have done the same for him as the Bannack woman did for her mate?

A quirk of the Dimsdale nature that must have baffled
Nettie was the odd combination of her husband's rather
prissy nature and the he-man roughness with which he reported conversations of road agents. In one paragraph there
would appear a delicate French phrase, and the next would
repeat the vile language of a Boone Helm. Of course, Tom
may have given Nettie the same explanation of this ability
to exactly quote the road agents that he gave in his book,
explaining this special skill of his as follows:

We have recorded a few, among many, of the crimes and
outrages that were daily committed in Bannack. The account
is purposely literal and exact. It is not pleasant to write of
blasphemous and indecent language, or to record foul and
horrible crimes, but, as the anatomist must not shrink from the
corpse, which taints the air as he investigates the symptoms and
examines the results of disease, so the historian must either tell
the truth for the instruction of mankind, or sink to the level of
a mercenary pander, who writes, not to inform the people but
to enrich himself!

Can't you just see Nettie's good, well-scrubbed face wrin-
kled by smiles of pride as she basks in her husband's no-
bility?

Somehow I have the feeling that Nettie made this little
man feel *tall*, and furnished him with an unlimited supply
of pride, and self-confidence. He liked his women noble,
hero-worshipping (nice if he could be the hero), and almost
invisible. Females belonged in the background, in Dimsdale's way of thinking. Ending this same theory, Dimsdale
wrote "From Blue Stockings, Bloomers and strong-minded
she-males generally, Good Lord, deliver us."

Of course, Dimsdale could have been writing bitterly
of Nettie when he mentioned his distaste for a *woman*
doing a man's work, for Nettie seemingly wandered
far abroad, helping in anything that needed a hand. She

might have irritated him by following paths he considered too progressive, unfeminine, generally lacking in the widely accepted smelling-salts-handkerchief-dropping-dainty-vapourish mores and modes of the day.

Or she could have inspired these expressed ideas of Dimsdale's by her gentleness, subservience, gentility, and her attitude of always looking up to her husband, humoring even his eccentricities. We're inclined to believe she followed the second line of action—sweet docility!

Dimsdale was not broad minded but he did have the curiosity, the determination, to write "things as he saw them." That no doubt accounts for his vivid descriptions of the hurdy-gurdy girls, the brothels, the dance halls, and some of the feminine characters who had become coarse and calloused in their pursuit of gold. He blames many of the shooting scrapes in the early Dance Houses on quarrels over women, sweethearts, hurdy-gurdy girls, and prostitutes.

But always you find Gentleman Tom reaching out for the better things of life, even in the rough-and-ready mining camp of Virginia City. He headed the literary society there. He organized a singing group. He helped put on the nicer town dances. Thus we feel certain that Nettie, his wife, must have been someone he was very proud to introduce at these affairs, to have as his assistant in his widely assorted activities.

Along with the other wives of Virginia City Vigilantes, Mrs. Dimsdale must have constantly battled fear—fear for her husband's safety. Because, although he was frail physically, morally he faced the turbulent, gun-shooting, knife-stabbing dangers of Virginia City without flinching, either editorially or physically.

Because of his frank, fearless articles, and his known

Vigilante activities, this gentle man had many enemies. And this Nettie Dimsdale must have known . . . as all wives intuitively sense any danger lurking near their husbands.

She, too, must have waited patiently, tremblingly, until the *Montana Post* was "put to bed," must have sighed with relief and uttered a prayer of gratitude when she heard his footsteps approaching late at night, or early in the morning if the Vigilante session had been long, if the paper an unusually large one.

On May 5, 1866, the *Montana Post* of Virginia City carried the following announcement on Page 3, Column 3:

MARRIED
On the 1st instance, at the residence of the bride, Virginia City, by Colonel Stafford, J. P., Professor T. J. Dimsdale, of the Montana Post, to Miss Annette Hotchkiss.

That's more brevity than T. J. ever used on his writings. Also, the date of Professor Dimsdale's death is given as September 22, 1866, by all reliable historians. Thus, if Annette and Thomas were not wed until May 1, 1866, they were only married some four months and a half when death did them part.

The Deer Lodge Montana paper, issue of August 29, 1874, published the most complete obituary of Annette Dimsdale Foster. This account claims that the then Annette Hotchkiss came to Virginia City, June 11, 1864, and that "shortly after her arrival she was married to Professor Thomas Dimsdale."

The *Weekly Montanian*, Virginia City, in its obituary of Mrs. Nettie Dimsdale Foster, printed August 20, 1874, stated that this Mrs. Foster came to Virginia City June 11, 1863. Perhaps this was a slip of the typesetter.

The three obituaries on Annette Hotchkiss Dimsdale Foster, are reprinted here exactly as we found them in the Library of the Historical Society of Montana:

(Deer Lodge) The *New North-West*, August 29, 1874.

DIED.

FOSTER—In Virginia City, Aug. 17, 1874, *Nettie H.* wife of A. H. Foster, aged thirty-eight years.

Deceased was the pioneer of her sex in Alder Gulch. She was the first white woman who settled in Virginia City, where she has resided since June 11, 1864. Mrs. Foster was also one of the pioneers of Colorado Territory, from whence she came to Montana. Shortly after arrival she was married to Prof. Thomas Dimsdale, then editor of the *Montana Post*, a gentleman of much educational brilliancy and worth. Living at Virginia during the reign of the Vigilantes, she was an eye witness to many of the wild scenes daily occurring, and had, perhaps, more experience in the hardships and excitements of pioneer life than any other woman in Montana. Brave and generous, she had many warm and true friends who will be pained to hear of her death. After the death of Prof. Dimsdale, in 1866, she married Mr. Foster. Rest in peace.

(Virginia City) The *Weekly Montanian*, August 20, 1874.

DIED

In this city, on the 17th inst., Nettie H., Wife of A. H. Foster, aged thirty-eight years. Brookville, Penn., papers please copy.

The deceased was the pioneer of her sex in Alder Gulch. She was the first white woman that settled in Virginia City, where she has always resided since June 11, 1863.

The *Helena Daily Herald*, August 22, 1874, page 3, column 4

DIED.

In Virginia City, August 17th, 1874, Nettie H., wife of A. H. Foster, aged thirty-eight years./Brookville, Pa., papers please copy./

As to the death of Professor Dimsdale, in the September 29, 1866, issue of the *Montana Post*, Virginia City, was a column-long editorial on Mr. Dimsdale. This tribute to the editor-historian also printed a beautiful resolution passed by the Masonic Lodge of Virginia City, of which Professor Dimsdale, at the time of his death, was Grand Orator. Two paragraphs from the editorial follow:

About two weeks previous to his decease he wrote the preface to his history of the Vigilantes which will be published within a short period. He brought to the editorial chair . . . a wonderful versatility of talent and ample store of knowledge, which had been derived from the perusal of a large number of books. The *Montana Democrat* and the exchanges that are printed in the *States and Territories,* which are bounded by the Rocky Mountains or the Pacific Ocean, have noticed in appropriate terms his death, and eulogized his memory.

Professor Dimsdale was born in England, and retained many of the characteristics of the subjects of the Queen. Although he was true in his love of the country of his adoption and earnestly upheld the principles of a republican government, he never forgot the land of his birth and the familiar scenes of his childhood. *He was married a few months since and leaves a widow to mourn his loss.* We publish the proceedings and resolutions of the Masonic Order, which will receive the hearty concurrence of all.*

At the very end of the resolution passed by the Masonic Lodge appear these two paragraphs:

RESOLVED. That we tender to his afflicted widow, the sympathies of the Masonic Fraternity of Virginia City, and commend her for consolation to the widow's God who "doeth all things well."

RESOLVED. That the Lodge be draped in mourning for the period of thirty days, that these resolutions be entered of record in the Lodge, that a copy thereof be sent by the Secretary under seal of the Lodge, to the widow of our departed brother, and that these proceedings be published in each of the papers of the City.

Both the editorial and the Masonic resolution give further proof that Professor Dimsdale was married at the time of his death although neither the editorial nor the resolution mention Mrs. Dimsdale by name, merely referring to her as "the widow."

In the brief death notice, also printed in the *Montana*

---

* Italics mine.

Post, Virginia City on September 22nd, 1866, there is no mention made of any survivors of Professor Dimsdale.

The fact that the *Montana Post* did not list Professor Dimsdale's wife in its obituary notice on September 22nd but did mention her in the long write-up in the *Montana Post* of September 29th makes one think that perhaps few in Alder Gulch knew of Professor Dimsdale's marriage to Annette Hotchkiss prior to his death.

Some of the old-timers contend that Professor Dimsdale was married in England before he came to Canada and Montana. But biographer after biographer allude to him as a bachelor.

We feel most definitely that this eulogistic column on Dimsdale in the *Montana Post* and on file in the Library of the Historical Society of Montana is additional proof of Dimsdale's marital status at the time of his death.

In *Golden Gulch—The Story of Montana's Alder Gulch,* a colorful book written by Dick Pace of Virginia City and published by Mr. Pace in 1962, there is a mention of Annette Hotchkiss Dimsdale Foster, but only by the name of Mrs. Foster. Mr. Pace wrote: "The first white woman arrived sooner than was usual for a new camp. Young Nettie H. Foster came with her husband June 11, to settle in the Gulch where she lived until her death August 17, 1874. Granville Stuart's wife is recorded to have had one of the first children, a daughter born October 6, 1863."

The June 11 referred to by Mr. Pace is accepted as June 1863, as he had been speaking of that date previously.

Using our imagination to pad out the meagre obituaries and marriage notice of Annette Hotchkiss Dimsdale Foster, we venture that she looked at life through the same philosophical spectacles as her husband. She might have been the big adventure in the life of Professor Thomas J. Dimsdale—an adventure that he shared with no one but his Nettie, the queen of his own very personal, carefully guarded private life. She may not have understood all the poetry he read to her, but it transported her to an exciting, spine-tingling world. She glowed when she realized that she had the power to make this little man, her man, *tall*. Her adventure, indeed, must have been far beyond her most tinselled day dreams.

9. Epilogue:

Again the Good Women

It was the good women of Virginia City—the very same ones who nine months earlier had gotten the murderers Stinson and Lyons freed—who signed the death warrant for "Cap" Joseph A. Slade and thus helped to bring abruptly to a close the most active work of the Montana Vigilantes. Frankly, this was a case where it would have been wiser for the women to attend to the housework and let their men-folks take care of the hangings.

Today throughout the west you can get an argument on the Slade hanging, any time, any place. You'll hear many an otherwise cool-headed, ardent booster of the old time Montana Vigilantes label the Slade hanging as "the one blunder of the Vigilantes." Banishment, yes; they all agree that Slade should have been turned out of the territory, but not "murdered." That his playmates in deviltry were not even arrested, let alone punished, makes these square-shooting westerners place another black mark against the fifty righteous hangmen, and often brings forth this comment: "It seems there had to be an example to show these swashbuckling lawbreakers that this lawlessness in disturbing the peace could not go on. Slade was the example."

In modern phraseology Slade was the "patsy," the "fall guy"; he took the "rap!"

However reluctant the husbands of Virginia City's good women may have been to subdue Slade, the warrant was out for him that night after his drunken appearance at the Virginia City theatre. It was composed at the general store, passed over the backyard fences, delivered ultimas ultimatum in flannel nightgowns by the stern-faced, tight-lipped women of the town.

Slade's hanging, which critics of that period and since have called a blunder which smirches the otherwise generally supported and justified crusade of the Montana Vigilante Committee, has many elements of irony, for he was not hanged for murder but for disturbing the peace—a pretty tough punishment for a peace disturber! And to this day, arguments go on as to whether "Cap" Slade was a hero or a knave, whether he was hanged or murdered.

Whenever raconteurs of frontier history gather in Montana, whether at range riders' get-togethers, stockmen's conventions, at round-ups or just "to hoist one" in a friendly bar, someone is certain to start an argument about Slade. Was he a rascal or a misunderstood leader? Didn't he inadvertently serve the cause of law and order in Montana by swinging from an improvised scaffold? Would the Vigilantes have continued as an active organization if they had merely banished Slade? Wasn't it dissension over this, their last decision—and even perhaps shame that they had hanged one of their former members—that broke up their organization? Or was his hanging necessary to create respect for western justice? Whatever the answer there is no doubt that the women of Bannack and Alder Gulch played a prominent part in the story of the Montana Vigilantes.

Not all the women—as I hope you've gleaned from this book—of Bannack, Virginia City, Junction, Nevada City, and generally Alder Gulch, were whores, or as the motion picture code has it "dance hall girls." As you have read, there was a sufficient number of good women in Alder Gulch to prevent the first sentence of hanging to be carried out (thereby causing the Vigilantes the necessity of doing it later) and, conversely, to goad their menfolk on to another hanging—Slade's.

We do not feel that all the virtuous women were really good in a charitable Christian way, nor were all the so-called "bad women" rotten through and through. Madame Dumont, underneath her brightly veneered, brittle exterior, had a generous heart that often beat in sympathetic three-quarter time. The kind deeds of Virginia Slade were recorded. Libby Collins detoured repeatedly from her own rough, bumpy road to help others, even though she had to look out for the Smith family first. Mrs. Sanders was by no means a prissy person, and she did not wear her goodness like a brilliant red cape.

All of which brings us to an account of this pioneer woman's broad-mindedness, a rather rare quality in those stern days. Mrs. Sanders and the Vails were next-door neighbors. The Plummers had lived in the honeymoon cottage prior to Electa's departure (who knows, perhaps Mrs. Sanders and the pretty young Plummer bride exchanged recipes for cornbread) and then Sheriff Plummer moved in with his in-laws after his wife left him. When Plummer was hanged, Francis M. Thompson (you'll recall he was the "bridesmaid" at the Plummer wedding on Sun River), a storekeeper in Bannack, broke the news to Mrs. Vail of her brother-in-law's untimely demise. Mrs. Vail fainted. Thompson rushed next door and called Mrs. Sanders, who cared for the grief-stricken Mrs. Vail. This was another of those classic ironies as Mrs. Sanders' husband, Wilbur, was the Vigilante prosecutor of the road agents, and he had turned aside Plummer's pleas for mercy at the foot of the gallows.

Then, consider the mores and modes of the so-called bad women of the Vigilante era. Living, even on the pioneer "primrose path," was not easy or luxurious.

The hurdy-gurdy girls never knew what kind of a man they'd have to dance with; as the men paid their money for tickets, the girls danced. Maybe it might be someone like J. H. Morley, a young man who kept a diary, read *Ivanhoe* and *David Copperfield,* and organized a literary society in Virginia City (although this young "intellectual" did have his moments when he strayed to billiard halls, bars, and dance establishments—according to his published diary, *The Road To Virginia City.* Or maybe it would be a road agent seeking relaxation after pulling off a stagecoach robbery and casually murdering a couple of men. Or the "gurdy's" partner might be one of the town's leading business men—a married man, too—slightly bored with domesticity and looking for a "little clean fun."

Professor Dimsdale gives an eye-witness account of these dance halls:

One "institution" offering a shadowy and dangerous substitute for more legitimate female association, deserves a peculiar notice. This is the "Hurdy-Gurdy" house. As soon as the men have left off work, these places are opened and dancing commences. Let the reader picture himself in a large room, furnished with a bar at one end where champagne at $12 (in gold) per bottle and "drinks" at twenty-five to fifty cents are wholesaled (correctly speaking)—and divided, at the end of this bar, by a railing running from side to side. The outer enclosure is densely crowded (and, on particular occasions, the inner side also) with men in every variety of garb that can be seen on the continent.

Beyond the barrier sit the dancing women, called "hurdy-gurdies," sometime dressed in uniform, but more generally habited, according to the dictates of individual caprice, in the finest clothes money can buy, and which are fashioned in the most attractive styles that fancy can suggest. On one side is a raised orchestra. The music suddenly strikes up, and the summons "take your partner for the next dance" is promptly answered by some of the male spectators, who, paying a dollar in gold for a ticket, approach the ladies' bench and—in style polite, or otherwise, according to antecedents—invite one of the ladies to dance.

The number being complete, the parties take their places, as in any other dancing establishment, and pause for the performance of the introductory notes of the air.

Let us describe a first class dancer—"sure of a partner every time"—and her companion. There she stands at the head of the set. She is of middle height, of rather full and rounded form; her complexion is as pure as alabaster, a pair of dangerous looking hazel eyes, a slightly Roman nose, a small and prettily formed mouth. Her auburn hair is neatly banded and gathered in a tasteful, ornamented net, with a roll and gold tassels at the side. How sedate she looks during the first figure, never smiling till the termination of "promenade, eight," when she shows her little white hands in fixing her handsome brooch in its place, and settling her glistening earrings. See how nicely her scarlet dress, with its broad black band round the skirt, and its black edgings, set off her dainty figure. No wonder that a wild mountaineer would be willing to pay—not one dollar, but all that he has in his purse—for a dance and an approving smile from so beautiful a woman.

Her cavalier stands six feet in his boots, which come to the knee and are garnished with a pair of Spanish spurs, with rowels and bells like young water wheels. His buckskin leggings are fringed at the seams, and gathered at the waist with a U. S. belt, from which hangs his loaded revolver and his sheath knife. His neck is bare, muscular, and embrowned by exposure, as is also his bearded face, whose sombre hue is relieved by a pair of piercing dark eyes. His long black hair hangs down beneath his wide felt hat, and in the corner of his mouth is a cigar, which rolls like the lever of an eccentric as he chews the end in his mouth.

After an amazingly grave salute, "all hands round" is shouted by the prompter, and off bounds the buckskin hero, rising and falling to the rhythm of the dance, with a clumsy agility and a growing enthusiasm testifying his huge delight. His fair partner, with practiced foot and easy grace, keeps time to the music like a clock, and rounds to her place as smoothly and gracefully as a swan. As the dance progresses, he of the buckskins gets excited, and nothing but long practice prevents his partner from being swept off her feet, at the conclusion of the miner's delight "set your partners" or "gents to the right."

An Irish tune or a horn-pipe generally finishes the set, and then the thunder of heel and toe, and some amazing demivoltes are brought to an end by the afore-said "gents to the right" and "promenade to the bar" which last closes the dance. After a treat, the barkeeper mechanically raps his blower as a hint to "weigh out," the ladies sit down, and with scarcely an interval, a waltz, polka, schottische, mazurka, varsovienne, or another quadrille commences.

All varieties of costume, physique, and demeanor can be noticed among the dancers—from the gayest colors and loudest styles of dress and manner, to the snugly fitted black silk and plain white collar, which sets off the neat figure of the blue-eyed, modest-looking Anglo-Saxon. Yonder, beside the tall and tastefully clad German brunette you see the short curls, rounded tournure, and the smiling face of an Irish girl; indeed, representatives of almost every dancing nation of white folks may be seen on the floor of the Hurdy-Gurdy house.

The earnings of the dancers are very different in amount. That dancer in the low-necked dress, with the scarlet "waist," a great favorite and really good dancer, counted fifty tickets into her lap before "The last dance, gentleman," followed by "only this one before the girls go home," which wound up the performance. Twenty-six dollars is a great deal of money to earn in such a fashion; but fifty sets of quadrilles and four waltzes, two of them for the love of the thing, is very hard work.

As a rule, however, the professional "hurdies" are Teutons, and, though first-rate dancers, they are with some exceptions the reverse of good-looking.

The dance which is most attended is one in which ladies to whom pleasure is dearer than fame represent the female element, and, as may be supposed, the evil only commences at the Dance House. It is not uncommon to see one of these sirens with an "outfit" worth from seven to eight hundred dollars, and many of them invest with merchants and bankers thousands of dollars in gold, the rewards and presents they receive, especially the more highly favored ones, being more in a week than a well-educated girl would earn in two years in an Eastern city.

In the Dance House you can see Judges, the Legislative corps, and every one but the Minister. He never ventures further than to engage in conversation with a friend at the door, and while intently watching the performance, lectures on the evil of such places with considerable force; but his attention is evidently more fixed upon the dancers than on his lecture. Sometimes may be seen gray-haired men dancing, their wives sitting at home in blissful ignorance of the proceeding. There was never a Dance House running, for any length of time, in the first days of a mining town, in which shooting scrapes do not occur; equal proportions of jealousy, whiskey, and revenge being the stimulants thereto.

As the respectable women of Alder Gulch had hardened during the months, so too the Vigilantes had become more rock-ribbed in their handling of the road agents, especially in barring women and their sentimental influence. The stern Vigilante order, "Men, do your duty," spoken just before the box was kicked out from under twenty-five murderers and the peace-disturber Slade, never fell on the horrified, womanly ears of any woman. To the Vigilantes, these hangings were grim business and not tea parties, hence their adamant ruling: "No women."

For instance when Haze Lyons was finally hanged, just before his execution he made one request, a request backed up by the shotguns and pistols of the Gulch's tougher element: He asked to be allowed to see his sweetheart, Cora, one of the camp's notorious "frail ladies."

But the sombre-faced Vigilantes, remembering back some nine months, refused his first and second request. Finally, when he pleaded for the third time to see Cora, he received this answer: "Haze! Emphatically *no!* By God, bringing women to the place of execution played out in '63. No women permitted at these hangings."

Lyons nodded philosophically, asked them to give Cora

the watch in his pocket, and also requested that she be allowed to have his body for burial.

At Bannack, when Ned Ray and Buck Stinson were at the foot of the gallows, Ray begged to be allowed to say farewell to his mistress, known as "Madame Hall." Ned Ray was the real dandy, the dude, the Beau Brummel of the Plummer gang. He was a tall, slender man with a sandy complexion, long red-brown hair falling over his shoulders. He wore the neatly trimmed mustache and goatee favored by Plummer's killers. His boots were knee-length and always highly polished. His squaw kept his linen immaculate, his boots polished, and his soft buckskin suits spotless. In fact, his squaw kept him looking like a fashion plate for his mistress, Madame Hall, a notorious courtesan of Bannack.

Following the hanging of Ray, Stinson, and Plummer the Vigilantes patrolled the area around the gallows, as the friends of the road agents had gathered and were thought to be planning trouble, even an attack on the Vigilantes.

Finally, loud groans and cries were heard in the vicinity of the scaffold, and a detail was assigned to investigate the noise. The detachment soon met Madame Hall who was "making the night hideous" with her doleful wailings. She insisted on knowing what had happened to her sweetheart, Ned Ray, and one of the Vigilantes said bluntly: "Well, if you must know, he is hung."

A volcanic eruption of oaths and abuse was her reply to this announcement; but the men were short on time— and disposition—and escorted her towards her dwelling without any Chesterfieldian gestures. She was rushed to her cabin and later claimed the body of her paramour.

Speaking again of the good and bad women of this era: A wedding ring became the token of many a so-called "loose" woman's reformation, the open-sesame to polite society. This story is from the lips of a Montana woman of those early days:

My next-door neighbor worked in a girl-house when she first came west. Her husband married her right out of that house and brought her out here. Come right down to it, what business did he have in a place like that, in the girl-house, any more than she did? What I always remember about that woman is that she baked the sweetest, whitest bread I ever put in my mouth. Then, too, she sat up all night for three nights running when my youngest took with diptheria and pulled him through as well as a doctor could have. They're the things worth remembering.

Another pioneer woman of the '60's offered this word of wisdom: "We never ask women where they come from or what they did before they came to live in our neck of the woods. If they wore a wedding band and were good wives, mothers, and neighbors that was enough for us to know. A marriage band with us has a way of stopping a lot of silly questions."

Also, the hurdy-gurdy girl of early Montana was not always a prostitute. Their activities stopped with dancing and drinking—some of them just sold drinks but did not imbibe themselves—and many of them went on to marry responsible, successful western men. The "gurdies" received commissions on the drinks and dances they sold, the dances in the better places selling for a dollar each, and the drinks from 25 cents to a dollar. For many of them, the day ended at the door of the dance hall. If a girl got paid for "other services," then she was more than a hurdy-gurdy girl, and there was another name for her and likewise her age-old profession.

Many socialites, prominent professional men, business leaders, cattle barons, mining millionaires, civic and political leaders, can trace their ancestry—and do—back to some hurdy-gurdy girl in Virginia or Nevada Cities or Bannack. And they do it pridefully, too, because they know what stalwart souls their feminine ancestors were, what respected women they were in the dance halls, in their homes, in their communities. The hurdy-gurdies may have had a gold flecked existence, but not an easy, gently upholstered one! Theirs too was a matter of *survival!*

For during the settlement of Montana, during those frightening, turbulent Vigilante days when brave men fought for law and order, the word carved on every woman's heart, whether she was rated good or bad, was SURVIVAL. To survive those rigorous journeys across the plains as Mrs. Sanders, Mrs. Plassman, and Mrs. Libby Smith Collins did took a stern, unbending will. Then, to keep house and make a life for a family in this wilderness or to earn a living tested the strongest soul. Libby Collins, Madame Dumont, Lucia Darling were the "career women" of those uncertain days on the Montana frontier. Even to dance and live and love among gambling, drinking, shooting, fighting men as Madame Dumont did called for an unusual brand of bravery, and a courage that didn't crumple at the sight of another dead gambler hitting the barroom floor, or another road agent swinging limply in the wintry wind.

Yes, survival is the word for the western women settlers because in the early sixties, out where the West began, the problem of survival confronted every woman. True, most women didn't know the meaning of the words frustration, complexes—inferiority or otherwise—social equality, careers for women, eternal triangle, Freud, calories, or malnutrition. They had neither a recognized problem of juvenile delinquency, nor washing machines, parent-teacher groups, beauty salons, or heaps of other conveniences which today we accept as "routine" blessings.

Few jobs were open to women in these new mining camps: school teaching, nursing, sewing, working in dance halls or as cooks or waitresses. And even these jobs were scarce as most of the business places were manned by the males of the town. Employment of "gurdies" in the dance halls and "dealers" in the gambling establishments rated next to marriage in those long-ago days. There were few schools so there was little demand for schoolmarms; also, few hospitals, so nursing was done mainly in the log homes. Dressmakers did their work at home, too.

The only break that women got in those frontier mining camps—and it was a dubious break—was the abundance of men, and the scarcity of women. In Alder Gulch there were 10,000 men and 100 respectable women, and most of those were married. In 1863 there were 1,000 men and 30 respectable women in Bannack. The "gurdies," the prostitutes, the gambling den girls, made up a fluctuating, floating population.

With no inside plumbing, no gas or electric lights or stoves, no furnaces, no vacuum cleaners or other such conveniences, and none of the "ready-mixes," or ice boxes, the women of Alder Gulch and Bannack in 1863–1864 really had a back-breaking chore keeping house. It must be that "the easy way," describing the life of demimondes, was coined in those early days on the western frontier, "easy" being a matter of stern comparisons in this rugged existence. Thus, to survive was the challenge that came automatically to every woman on the frontier.

Treating the expression to a bit of refinement, one might imagine that the advice given by a fond father to his daughter was: "Go West, young woman, but take your heavy underwear and intestinal fortitude with you!"

One must consider shifting scenes, shifting values in judging and evaluating the Vigilante woman! And who can deftly paint a portrait, a true portrait, a finished portrait of her. She's been reproduced in tight-bodiced, full-skirted satin gowns, and hats weighted down with willow plumes. She's smiled wanly from heavy gold frames, her dress long-skirted and of calico, her sunbonnet drooping and faded.

But the Vigilante woman was far more than a painted face under the lacy shadows of willow plumes; more even than a sweet, tired, colorless face peering from under a shabby sunbonnet. There was more of character than mere prettiness in the faces of these women. The song of home hummed incessantly in their hearts whether it was a frame, two-story dwelling like that occupied by Mrs. Wilbur Fisk Sanders in Virginia City (one of the two frame houses at that time in that town), a one-room cabin with a dirt floor and no door in which Libby Smith lived when she first came to Virginia City, or the stone house in which Virginia Slade dwelt with her romantic but roistering husband, or even the tiny rooms occupied by the Virginia City hurdy-gurdies. Home was what all these women of the frontier desired and placed high on their list of cherished possessions.

So we ask you, before finishing this book, to create your own picture of a Vigilante woman. We urge you to make it a composite portrait, for we feel certain, after delving for years into the lives and loves and perils of the Vigilante women, that the real, the typical woman of these soul-testing times had some of the characteristics of each of our six heroines. Consider:

The steely courage it took for Electa Bryan Plummer to leave her handsome Henry. He no doubt fascinated and charmed her, and she loved him, but she knew that staying with a man with clay feet and bloody hands would only destroy her, so she conquered her great, burning love through flight.

The good deeds of Libby Smith while she battled valiantly to succeed personally. Candles were expensive in those days, and not plentiful either, but figuratively Libby seemed always to be holding one of those candles in her hand, the light throwing a far beam into a naughty, bafflingly snarled-up world.

The tranquil, serene, yet valiant life of Harriett Sanders, unaffected by those turbulent times, not condemning those who lived high, wide, and handsome. She had that milk of human kindness that sent her scurrying to the side of those in need, whether they were good or bad, on this side or that of the main street.

The zest for living, the patient and never-weakening loyalty, the fierce sympathy of Maria Virginia Slade, who stayed faithful and respectable when bolstered up by love, but who slid to the depths when both her dreams and her lover, "Cap" Slade, died. And that deep tragedy when she arrived half-dead on her exhausted black stallion, with her hair drifting like an ominous black cloud behind her, and her husband, the only man she ever loved, dead, having died in disgrace at the end of a rope.

The ever-bubbling fountain of inspiration that was the rare characteristic of Lucia Darling, Montana's first schoolmarm, her briskly stimulating nature having a contagious cheeriness. Taking adventure where she found it with a naiveté that even cowed an overhung drunk resting under his buffalo robes. When she crossed the plains and was on night-watch with her gun across her knees, she thought more of the willows swaying in the moonlight than she did of hostile Indians or snarling wolves. She liked to lead the singing in that first little log Montana school house rather than gaze morbidly on the ghostly gallows. Mark up a generous dash of idealism for Lucia!

The honesty of Madame Eleanore Dumont as she met the debt she need not have paid; her generosity as she loaned a miner, a down-and-outer, a poke of gold dust so that he could make a new start, while at the same time looking around for a prospector who'd just struck it rich, thus enabling her to replenish her funds—the virtual feminine Robin Hood of the frontier!

Annette Dimsdale, whose full life but brief life history puzzles researchers and baffles historians.

The Vigilante woman, whether good or bad—and who was there to cast stones, especially when there were so many nuggets shining here, there, and everywhere—was straightforward, usually honest and generous, and always looking for life, liberty, and the happiness of pursuit. Her face may have been painted none too subtly or it may have been leathery from hard living and trying elements, but no veneer dominated the countenance of a woman of the early West. She lived and loved and worked and dared immense dangers with an indestructible gusto, a never lessening energy.

Bibliography

BOOKS

Adams, Ramon F. *The Rampaging Herd*. Norman, Oklahoma: University of Oklahoma Press, 1959.

Aikman, Duncan. *Calamity Jane and the Lady Wildcats*. New York: Henry Holt & Co., 1927. A later edition was published around 1957 by Blue Ribbon Books, Inc.

Birney, Hoffman. *Vigilantes*. Philadelphia: Penn Publishing Company, 1928.

Collins, Mrs. Nathaniel (Libby Smith). *Cattle Queen of Montana or The Cowboys' Mother*. Compiled by CHARLES WALLACE. Chicago: Donohue and Henneberry, 1894. Edited by ALVIN E. DYER and reprinted by the Dyer Printing Company Press, Spokane, Washington, in 1902. (The 1894 edition, written by Mrs. Collins and compiled by Mr. Wallace, is very rare, as Mr. Wallace burned more than 1,000 copies of the book, which he regretted vastly. It is found now only in Rare Book Sections of a few libraries, including the New York Public Library.)

Dimsdale, Thomas J. *The Vigilantes*. First serialized in the *Montana Post*, Virginia City, Montana, in 1865 and 1866. Then published in book form by this paper in 1866. Third edition, edited by A. J. NOYES, published by the State Publishing Company, Helena, Montana, 1911;

fourth edition, edited by B. E. Calkins, published by the Butte *Miner,* Butte, Montana, 1921; fifth edition, with Foreword by E. DeGolyer, published by the University of Oklahoma Press, Norman, Oklahoma, in 1953, with second, third and fourth printings in 1954, 1955, and 1956 by Oklahoma Press in their "The Western Frontier Library" series.

Brown, Dee. *The Gentle Tamers, Women of the Old Wild West.* New York: G. P. Putnam's Sons, 1958.

Gard, Wayne. *Frontier Justice.* Norman, Oklahoma: University of Oklahoma Press, 1949.

Haycox, Ernest. *Alder Gulch.* Boston: Little, Brown & Company, March 1942; serialized by *Collier's* Magazine in 1941–42; republished by Grosset & Dunlap in February 1947, with second printing in September 1948, third printing in August 1953. Bantam Books Edition, October 1961.

Henry, Will. *Reckoning at Yankee Flats.* New York: Random House, 1958. Bantam Books Edition, 1959.

Howard, Helen Addison. *Northwest Trail Blazers.* Caldwell, Idaho: Caxton Printers, Ltd., 1963.

Howard, Joseph Kinsey. *Montana Margins, a State Anthology.* New Haven, Conn.: Yale University Press, 1946.

Johnson, Dorothy M. *Vigilante Days and Ways.* Re-edited and with a Foreword by Miss Johnson and republished by the University of Montana Press at Missoula, Montana, 1958 from the original manuscript by Nathaniel P. Langford.

Langford, Nathaniel P. *Vigilante Days and Ways.* New York: D. D. Merrill & Company, 1913. Republished in 1958 (see above).

Pace, Dick. *Golden Gulch, the Story of Montana's Fabulous*

Alder Gulch. Illustrated by SINDY COSENS. Published by Mr. Pace at Virginia City, Montana, 1962.

Sanders, Helen Fitzgerald. *History of Montana*. 3 vols. Chicago: Lewis Publishing Company, 1913.

Sanders, Helen Fitzgerald, in collaboration with William Bertsche, Jr., published by the University of Oklahoma Press, Norman, Oklahoma, 1957.

Stone, Irving. *Men to Match My Mountains*. New York: Doubleday & Company, 1956.

Stuart, Granville. *Forty Years on the Frontier*. 2 vols. Cleveland, Ohio: Arthur H. Clark Company, 1925.

Toole, Ross. *An Uncommon Land*. Norman, Oklahoma: University of Oklahoma Press, 1959.

Twain, Mark. *Roughing It*. 2 vols. Hartford, Connecticut: American Publishing Company, 1871, 1903, 1915. Also, some listings give James R. Osgood, Boston, Mass., as publisher of *Roughing It* in 1872.

LETTERS

Harvey, Daniel. A letter written in 1934 by Mr. Harvey, of Buffalo, New York, and published at that time in a Buffalo paper, in which he describes a meeting with Madame Eleanore Dumont, one-time gambling queen of the west.

Meredith, Emily Robertson. Letters written by Mrs. Meredith in the spring of 1863 from Bannack, Montana, to relatives in Maryland and to friends and relatives in Minnesota.

Slattery, Mrs. John. A letter written by Mrs. Slattery to the Montana State Historical Society in July 1930. Mrs. Slattery, of Wakonda, South Dakota, a step-daughter of Mrs. John Maxwell, the widow of Sheriff Henry Plummer, hanged by the Montana Vigilantes, revealed in this letter the whereabouts of Mrs. Plummer after she fled Plummer. Mrs. Plummer married John Maxwell, helped raise his children, of whom Mrs. Slattery was one, and is buried at Wakonda, S. D.

Thompson, Francis M. A letter written in June 1863 by Mr. Thompson to Mr. Joseph Swift, Jr., describing the wedding of Sheriff Henry Plummer and Miss Electa Bryan, on June 20, 1863, at St. Peter's Mission, Montana. Thompson was best man for Plummer, and remained devoted to the rascal lawman even as Plummer mounted the gallows.

(All these letters are now in the archives of the Montana State Historical Library at Helena, Montana. Included is also a series of letters written by Mrs. Meredith, who, with her sister, were the first two graduates of Hamline University, in 1859.)

DIARIES

Darling, Lucia. Her diary, *Crossing the Plains,* written in the spring and summer of 1863. Miss Darling was Montana's first school teacher.

Morley, J. H. A diary written at Virginia City, Montana, in 1863.

Miller, James Knox Polk. Edited by ANDREW F. ROLLE under the title *The Road to Virginia City.* Published by the University of Oklahoma Press, Norman, Oklahoma, 1960.

Sanders, Harriett (Mrs. Wilbur Fisk Sanders). Written when the Sanderses crossed the plains from Ohio, to Bannack, Montana, in 1863.

(All of these diaries now in the possession of the Montana State Historical Library, Helena, Montana.)

RECORDS

A resolution passed by the Virginia City, Montana, Masonic Lodge at the time of Thomas J. Dimsdale's death, September 1866, and expressing sympathy to the late Mr. Dimsdale's widow, Annette Hotchkiss Dimsdale (later Mrs. Al Foster), although numerous writers still allude to Mr. Dimsdale as "a bachelor."

Marriage of Virginia Slade, widow of "Cap'n" Joseph A. Slade, executed by the Montana Vigilantes, recorded at Virginia City, March 22, 1865. On that date Widow Slade married J. M. Kiskadden of Salt Lake City in a ceremony performed by Judge H. S. Hosmer, Chief Justice of the Montana Supreme Court.

Marriage of Thomas J. Dimsdale and Miss Annette Hotchkiss on May 1, 1866. Record filed at Virginia City, Montana, and published in the *Montana Post,* May 1, 1866. Marriage performed by Justice of the Peace Colonel Stafford in Virginia City, Montana.

(All papers and announcements are in the Montana Historical Library archives.)

NEWSPAPER ARTICLES

Chicago *Drovers' Journal,* Chicago, October 1891. Article on Mrs. Nathaniel (Libby Smith) Collins, the "Cattle Queen of Montana."

Montana Post. Numerous articles published in this paper during the years 1864, 1865, and 1866. The *Montana Post,* founded in Virginia City in 1864, was Montana's first full-fledged newspaper. This was the paper of which Thomas J. Dimsdale was editor and which ran his series of articles on "Vigilantes of Montana," which was later published by the *Montana Post* in book form.

New Northwest, Deer Lodge, Montana, August 29, 1874.

Weekly Montanian, Virginia City, August 20, 1874.

The Montanian, Choteau, Montana, 1894 and 1895. Articles about Mrs. Nathaniel (Libby Smith) Collins.

Montana News Association Inserts on reminiscences of Lucia Darling, Montana's first school teacher, published at intervals in the late 1890's and 1900's.

Helena *Daily Herald,* Helena, Montana, August 22, 1874.

The Bodie *Free Press,* Bodie California, September 1879. An article on the death of Madame Eleanore Dumont.

The Butte *Miner,* Butte, Montana, September 1879. Front page article and editorial on the death of Madame Eleanore Dumont, notorious woman gambler, who died in Bodie, California.

Newspaper columns and lengthy feature stories written by Martha Edgerton Plassman, daughter of Montana's first territorial governor. These pieces were published in the Helena *Record,* Helena, Montana; the Butte *Miner,* Butte, Montana; the Great Falls *Tribune,* Great Falls, Montana; *The Montanian,* Choteau, Montana; also in the Bozeman and Missoula, Montana, newspapers. Her articles appeared over a period from just before the turn of the century to the late twenties.

Article by Supreme Court Justice Llewellyn L. Calloway on "Cap'n" Joseph Slade published in Montana papers at turn of the century. Given special attention in the Butte *Miner,* Butte, Montana.